W9-CNN-836

MEANT TO LIVE

ENDORSEMENTS for *Meant to Live* by Nancy Hicks

"When I first met Nancy Hicks she floored me with her enthusiasm! Her love for God encouraged and inspired me. Our connection drew me closer to her intimacy with the God of the Universe. You, like I, can be running over with the love of God and the joy of a relationship with Him when you read the epic book written by my friend, Nancy Hicks. As she speaks you will want to listen. You can fall in Love with Jesus by reading Nancy's heart!"

Dr.Thelma Wells, D.D., Founder of A Woman of God Ministries,

Author, International speaker, professor

"This book is filled with good stories, good advice and good Biblically based theology. Even though it was written by someone who's life is committed to empowering women for leadership, men will find the book a very practical guide for living the Christian life in today's world."

Tony Campolo, PhD., Professor Emeritus, Eastern University

"*Meant to Live* is full of Nancy Hicks' authentic expression of following Jesus with fervor. It is her deep, deep desire for followers of Jesus to live out their faith with passion and purpose. But I "warn" you: Nancy's enthusiasm is contagious!"

Bob Snyder MD, President, IHS Global

"The glory of God is reserved for God alone. It's strange how this statement can actually cause God's people to pull back and stand down. But Nancy unpacks this theological matter in a very accessible way and helps us rise up and come alive. Read her defense for God's glory in His people. We need more female leaders writing from this perspective today."

Suellen Roberts,
Founder and President of Christian Women in Media Association

"Complacent Christianity is all around us… and in us. Nancy takes us on her vulnerable journey to authentically being 'awake and alive in Christ for life'! Don't miss this!"

Mary Beth Roe, QVC TV Host

"How do we recover from this mad malady of passive faith? We need a remedy. And there is one —it's Fire. Holy fire comes in a prophetic utterance, a burning bush, a raging cadence of a deep ancient hymn. It's in the soft voice of a child calling you back to yourself, camel-haired, wild men preaching in deserts, and, it turns out, in Nancy Hicks. A Canadian/American soprano soloist, TV personality, wife and mother, speaker and teacher infused with a God-breathed calling. She's got a passion to set us all on fire for God!"

Danielle Strickland
Author, international speaker, and founder of Communications, Inc.

MEANT TO LIVE

Living in Light of the Good News

Nancy Hicks

NASHVILLE

NEW YORK • LONDON • MELBOURNE • VANCOUVER

MEANT TO LIVE

Living in Light of the Good News

© 2020 Nancy Hicks

All rights reserved. No portion of this book may be reproduced, stored in a retrieval system, or transmitted in any form or by any means—electronic, mechanical, photocopy, recording, scanning, or other—except for brief quotations in critical reviews or articles, without the prior written permission of the publisher.

Published in New York, New York, by Morgan James Publishing. Morgan James is a trademark of Morgan James, LLC. www.MorganJamesPublishing.com

ISBN 9781642793284 paperback
ISBN 9781642793291 eBook
Library of Congress Control Number: 2018912803

Cover Design by:
Rachel Lopez
www.r2cdesign.com

Interior Design by:
Christopher Kirk
www.GFSstudio.com

Scripture quotations are from The Holy Bible, New International Version. Copyright © 1973, 1978, 1984 by International Bible Society.

Scripture taken from The Message. Copyright © 1993, 1994, 1995, 1996, 2000, 2001, 2002. Used by permission of NavPress Publishing Group.

Quote from Tucker Sweeney used by permission of Toi Sweeney in October 2018.

Lyrics quoted from "Survival Plan," by Wallace and Rachel Faagutu, featuring Samson. Copyright © 2009 Nutu. All rights reserved. Used by permission.

"The Cross Chart," found in *Sonship*, created by Jack Miller. Used with permission by New Growth Press.

Morgan James is a proud partner of Habitat for Humanity Peninsula and Greater Williamsburg. Partners in building since 2006.

Get involved today! Visit
MorganJamesPublishing.com/giving-back

For Gloria

Table of Contents

Foreword xi

Introduction 1

Part 1: Glory Lost

Chapter 1: The Church Alive 7

Chapter 2: Genesis. 11

Chapter 3: Bad News, Good News. 13

Chapter 4: The Untapped. 23

Chapter 5: Truth Protectors 35

Chapter 6: Keepin' It Reals. 47

Chapter 7: #Blessed 55

Chapter 8: Rag Rights 65

Chapter 9: Where Are You? 69

Part 2: Living in Light of the Good News

Chapter 10: Core Calling. 77

Chapter 11: How Then Shall We Live?. 81

Chapter 12: The Power of the Cross 87

Chapter 13: Get Honest. 95

Chapter 14: Curses. 105

Chapter 15: Blessings...................................111

Chapter 16: Excellence................................119

Part 3: The Struggle

Chapter 17: It's Risky................................131

Chapter 18: Humility................................139

Chapter 19: Suffering...............................151

Part 4: All Rise

Chapter 20: The Glorious One......................159

Chapter 21: I See! 167

Chapter 22: Arise, Shine 173

Chapter 23: A Glory Story.........................177

Foreword

By Danielle Strickland, author, international speaker, and founder of Communications, Inc.

Jesus came with good news. It's hard for us to fathom this sometimes because religious controls and our best intentions have been putting restraints on good. We manage to stifle the flame to a faint glimmer. Passion becomes a fleeting wish, our faith turns ever so slightly to pagan luck, and before we know it, we've confused Mary Poppins' best advice and reversed her recipe! Instead of putting sugar in the medicine to help it go down, we've ended up lacing the sugar with religious, sentimental poison. And it's killing us. Somehow the Western Church took the good news and missed its intention, swallowing a concoction that keeps us painfully stuck. And if we don't get some help soon it could actually do us in. This isn't just a big-picture corporate problem, it's an individual issue.

I've just returned from Rwanda, the site of one of the most monstrous acts of violence in this century. The Rwandan Genocide (where over a million people were violently massacred in forty days) happened on a Wednesday. The Sunday before, over 90% of Rwandans were in church. That statistic is unnerving. And I'd love to think that it's just a random happenstance, or a specific cultural issue that relates only to "them" and not to "us." But I'd miss the lesson. The truth here is a tough one to swallow, but essential to learn as soon as possible. Faith is not meant to be a humdrum rehearsal of creeds and beliefs divorced from actions, values, and relationships. Faith, as it was first embodied in God's people throughout Scripture, and personified in Jesus Himself, is a transforming presence of Hope, Truth, Grace, and Love that impacts our whole lives and everyone connected to us.

To be people of faith means to be lit up with the fiery vision of a whole world redeemed and transformed into a mutually flourishing global community. But if we are honest, this is not what is happening. Far from living the dream of God's Kingdom coming to earth, we retreat into a personal kind of faith. This kind of faith doesn't even penetrate our own problems, relationships, actions, beliefs, or connections, never mind reach the deepest needs of the world. We're not lit up with a fiery vision. We're lukewarm.

The reasons lukewarm faith is not OK are plentiful. It's not God's dream for your life. Jesus came to give us so much more, something ALIVE with the elements of faith that can transform your deepest darkness into a shining light. Even your most vulnerable weaknesses can be used by a living faith to provide healing and hope! But it's not only *your* life that needs the impact of a passionate faith—it's the people around you. It's your family, neighbors, friends, the marginalized and excluded in your own town, city, and country. It's the global community that is fractured most severely when people just don't care to get involved. Your personal faith might possibly get you to church—but it won't change the world.

What can we do? How do we recover from this mad malady of passive faith? We need a remedy. And there is one. An age-old, classic recipe for dead religion—it's Fire. Holy fire comes in a prophetic utterance, a burning bush, a raging cadence of a deep ancient hymn. It's in the sweet, cool breeze of wind at the peak of a mountain climbed. It's in the soft voice of a child calling you back to yourself, camel-haired, wild men preaching in deserts, and, it turns out, in Nancy Hicks. A Canadian/American soprano soloist,

TV personality, wife and mother, speaker and teacher infused with a God-breathed calling. She's got a passion to set us all on fire for God!

If you are tired of the humdrum realities of a weak and flailing faith, you may just want to buckle your seatbelt and read this fiery flamethrower of a book. Nancy holds no punches, and why should she? She has somehow uncovered the original Good News recipe and offers it as a remedy for our weary souls. With no apologies, she comes armed with Truth, and applies Grace like Poppins does sugar. It does more than make the medicine go down—what results is akin to spiritual surgery.

Nancy systematically removes the barriers, beliefs, and patterns that have made us sick. Identifying and discarding the infected bits ensures we won't die, but how can true spiritual health return to our hearts? For us to live glorious, free, and abundant lives, Nancy offers us an ancient and truly relevant spiritual cure—resurrection. God offers us what He has always offered His beloved bride—a heart transplant. And that new heart pumps fresh blood through our veins. And our beaming Father breathes us back to life again.

It turns out the Truth *is* what sets us free and lights us up. It's not only a remedy for our own souls, it is a balm for the deepest hurts and needs of the world. I'm believing and praying that this book will help ignite a fire in the soul of the Church. As Nancy so beautifully puts it, we have good news that matches the hour.

So read and apply this book filled with practical instructions for an eternally fire-fueled life. Then live it out. It's going to be glorious.

Introduction

I once heard author and social critic Os Guinness say that our primary calling is to know God and make Him known.[1] This struck me as profound and thrilling. Knowing—seeing, hearing, and enjoying—God. Then letting that spill out all over the place—on people who agree with that and on those who don't. What a privilege and a high calling.

That's what we're all about. It's life.

The life of Jesus Christ in His people is a glorious thing! Tapping into that life and operating as we were meant to as the Church, His Body, is euphoric.

The Church

Over the centuries, the Church has lived and died for this great cause of life in Christ. We have preached and proclaimed, taught and explained God's love demonstrated in Christ's life, death, and resurrection. We have spoken with passion, often at the expense of family, financial stability, comfort, and life itself. Christians have understood the apostle Paul's emphatic assertion: *"For to me, to live is Christ and to die is gain"* (Philippians 1:21).

And there's nothing like God's people lovingly walking it out. Putting our words into action. We put on our working boots and hit the turf. Together. The Church in full force builds where there's been destruction. We feed, clothe, and care for the hungry and broken. The Church has always known that faith without works is dead (James 2:26).

Christ's mission to build His Church has not changed. But its people have.

Did You Know?

The Majority World (South America, Africa, Asia) is bursting with the Good News of God's love through Christ like never before in history. There are fantastic reports from around the globe of people coming to know God. Hundreds of thousands of people *daily* are responding to God's call to life.

But in western culture (North America and Western Europe), the opposite is true. Generally, Christians are floundering. Churches are dying. Christians are often unclear about what this call to life actually looks like on a day-to-day basis. It's as though the Gospel (literally translated as "Good News") hasn't quite gotten through.

Camping Out

In an effort to help get us unstuck and moving toward our glorious call in Christ, I've begun to get focused with Christians on some good news. In this book I share principles—about getting honest with ourselves and each other, about curses and blessings, and about living in excellence. These are principles that have made and continue to make a tremendous difference in my life. Everything I share is out of my experience in implementing these things for transformation. It's why I've taught and shared this material with countless people everywhere.

Also, I explain how I see so many of us Western Christians falling into four "camps": The Untapped, the Truth Protectors, the Keepin' It Reals and #Blessed.

While it's not a science by any means, the illuminating process can help us, as Christians, see our strengths and weaknesses—and potential. When I've personally gotten honest about these leanings, it's been tremendously freeing. That's why I want to share them with you.

The Gospel is God's call to a glorious life. It's the core calling: You were meant to live. To be utterly glorious! It's a tragedy and a gross oversight when followers of Jesus—Christians—don't live into that inherent glory. That's what we want to explore in this book.

My Call to Life

I am passionate about Jesus Christ. I have been for as long as I can remember. Spending my life in communication, most notably as a spokesperson on QVC, I've always led in the church, loving Jesus and His people. That love combo shows the world God's magnificence.

I was following Christ's call in his church and at QVC, when next thing I knew, God sent me to seminary to spend the rest of my life preaching and teaching about Him. He's given me a fervor to raise up women around the globe: Those who are oppressed. Those without hope. Those who struggle to grasp the kind of life God has called them into. Women without access to leadership training and biblical teaching.

And as a Canadian who now also holds an American passport, my heart aches for the spiritual state of North America. I'm a devoted follower of Christ, desperate to see Him exalted through the Gospel penetrating lives. But we're missing something. We're missing our calling.

When I look back on my life, I can see God's fingerprints and smudge marks (from those times I squirmed a bit) directing and leading me. He has called me into a life of proclaiming His name through whatever means I can. That's why I've written this book.

If there's one thing I want you to take away from this offering, it's this: through Jesus Christ, you're invited to become fully alive, now and forever.

"The glory of God is [YOU] fully alive." —*St. Irenaeus of Lyons*

Part 1

GLORY LOST

"A man can no more diminish God's glory by refusing to worship Him than a lunatic can put out the sun by scribbling the word, 'darkness' on the walls of his cell." —C. S. Lewis

CHAPTER 1

The Church Alive

"I came so they can have real and eternal life, more and better life than they ever dreamed of." John 10:10, The Message

How Much Longer?

How much longer? I wondered, as we made the lengthy drive from the frenzied, East Asian city to a rural church. I was feeling carsick. The combination of the summer heat, no air-conditioning, and sitting in the back seat—never good for me on long rides—set me up. There'd been no time for lunch, either.

"We've got to get to the church."

This Sunday marked the end of my two-week journey in this nation that was alive with the Good News of Jesus Christ.

My host, an energetic pastor, undauntedly forged ahead as he had for years. I was certainly not going to complain. By God's grace, I'd keep up.

Finally the car stopped.

"Here we are," he announced.

I stood, staring out at acres of wide-open, dusty land. "Where's the church?"

"There." He pointed way, way out.

I was grateful I didn't turn an ankle as we traipsed over unruly terrain for several minutes. "Oh, and by the way, there are no toilets, so . . ."

So, hold it or squat in the field, I figured. Got it.

Then there it was: a cinder block structure the size of most American elementary school gymnasiums. It had a corrugated green tin roof. Loud, indigenous, life-infused music flowed from within.

I was led to the doorway, and stepped inside.

My eyes welled up with tears.

Over two hundred dark-skinned, bright-eyed, new followers of Jesus stood on the dusty ground. I was struck by the colors of their clothing: red, yellow, regal purples and brilliant blues. Truly striking. Women and children were on one side of the room, men on the other.

We worshiped loudly. The adoration in their heart language was full of life, full of glory. There were no barriers. Instead, guttural voices, lively eyes, clapping hands, and happy hearts.

They came to celebrate that the Word of Life had come to their land. It was exhilarating to see the church so alive!

In The Village

Earlier that morning, we'd worshiped with another church in a village. One teenage girl prayed aloud for several minutes, just yearning, pleading, crying out to God to move and pour out His Spirit. "More, God. More!" She'd cried out in her own language, leading her brothers and sisters in Christ. They audibly joined her cry for more.

During tithes and offerings, I'd watched as a woman brought bags of grain to lay on the table. After worship, we all sat on the ground eating lunch together. I wondered if the woman's grain had been used to feed us that day. I was given a sneak peek at the men cooking, sitting on the floor in a small passageway just inside the church building. *Look how they work together,* I thought. It was so communal. A verse came to mind, ". . . *they ate together with glad and sincere hearts praising God and enjoying the favor of all the people*" (Acts 2:46, 47).

This pastor-friend who travelled with me had faced death in bringing the Gospel to that village. His great big, toothy grin never dimmed as he recounted the story of a gunman who threatened him when he wouldn't stop preaching this message of Life. With the gun held to his head, he'd bravely told the angry man, "You do what your god tells you to do, and I'll do what my God tells me to do."

Just how many stories had he gathered over the years? He actively joined God in His call to all people to come alive. He planted churches all across his nation—north, south, east, and west—with no plans of slowing down, despite the government's harshness toward Christianity.

"God is just too amazing. The Good News of Jesus Christ is spreading like wildfire here. God is calling my people and there's much work to be done!"

I saw that first hand.

Back At Home

After two weeks in that Asian country, I felt an increased desire for the life of the church in North America. I felt a bit like my pastor-friend who'd said, *God's just too amazing.* They're gloriously alive there. I just won't believe He's no longer calling people here at home.

But I thought about our comfort and entitlement. I weekly read articles of the church's decline, and ways to solve our un-churched and de-churched problems. I've experienced the general apathy. On the one hand, we're bored with too much time on our hands, lacking vision and purpose. On the other hand, we're busier than ever. Spinning. Separated. Cynical.

My mind wanders back to that one Asian country. I think about Priscilla, this lovely teenage girl. Alert, awake, and ready for action. She wanted God. She wanted to know everything she could about how God desires to make great use of her one life to live.

I wanted to scoop her up and bring her home with me. Home to the church in America. Pricilla didn't need lessons on loving God. She gets that! I thought perhaps the best use of my missions dollars would be to fly her to my church in suburban Philadelphia. What could it look like to put her up in front of our busy, distracted teens and have her explain how Jesus Christ changed everything for her and her family? What could it look like for Priscilla to passionately express how she's no longer without dignity or purpose? How everything she is and wants to be is for God and His phenomenal glory?

She knows God has called her. She's wide awake.

CHAPTER 2

Genesis

"But the Lord called to the [wo]man . . ." Genesis 3:9

There is a calling on all creation.

We see it in the very beginning of the Scriptures. "In the beginning," God shared breath and life with Adam and Eve. In the Garden, they ate, rested, created, and explored. They shared laughs. Together they walked along dreamy, green garden paths in the cool of the day. They shared a beautiful exchange of life and love.

God, who initiated this life-bond, gave Adam and Eve—His pinnacle of creation—responsibilities. Opportunities to join with Him in nurturing life. They cared for creation, including naming the animals and enjoying the fish and birds in the sea and sky. With God, they shared stories and dreams and the most imaginative ideas. For pleasure, Adam and Eve enjoyed the deepest physical act of intimacy so they could produce more little Adams and Eves. They were naked in every way and felt no shame. It was relational perfection.

All was well in the Garden, until . . .

In Genesis 3, Adam and Eve, God's masterfully engineered creatures, fraternized with the enemy. They ate the forbidden fruit. And death fell on them.

In the next scene we see God missing His usual companions: *"Then the man and his wife heard the sound of the LORD God as He was walking in the garden in the cool of the day, and they hid from the LORD God among the trees of the garden. But the LORD God called to the man, 'Where are you?'"* (Genesis 3: 8-9).

That's the scene.

This was the fall of creation through one man and one woman. Ashamed of their nakedness, Adam and Eve ran from God and ducked behind the bushes. They went into hiding.

But notice God. God went out and called, "Where are you?"

"Where Are You?"

He's calling us today as he did in the Garden in Genesis, after Adam and Eve had gone their own way. When they separated from God—who is life—for the first time ever, God called to them: "Where are you?"

Implicit in the text is the core calling that emerges from the scene and reverberates throughout all Scripture: You were meant to live!

CHAPTER 3

Bad News, Good News

Glorious: adj.
1. Having a striking beauty or splendor.
2. Excellent, exceptionally lovely, magnificent.[2]

I fidgeted in my seat. At ten years old, I loved to sing, but I wrestled with pre-performance jitters. My mom knew better. Whether it was in church, concert, or competition, Mom would lean over, and just before I'd leave my seat, she'd whisper, "Give the glory to God, Nancy."

Growing up, singing became a centerpiece of my life. Mom watched me gain strength up front while soloing in concert halls and churches, primarily in Canada. At home, she'd listen to me practice. She'd watch me work through songs and technical issues and memorize difficult passages. Mom would belly laugh with delight as I flitted around the house acting out a song, dramatic and silly. She loved to watch me do the "singer" things. She enjoyed watching me soar. Then she'd take it to a whole new level with the words: "Give Him the glory, child."

Mom said those words to me over and over at every stage of my life right before I stepped up to open my mouth.

It's probably why today I'm so passionate about glory. I am bold to say to just about any who'll listen: "Look up. Be inspired. Be awed. Be who God has called and created you to be. No more, no less. Then be grateful you have a part in revealing Him."

When we take this in, it changes us. We want this. It's why we experience an "uplift" and tears spring to our eyes when we hear songs like "You Raise Me Up" or when we read passages like: *"They that wait upon the Lord will renew their strength. They will mount up with wings as eagles ..."* (Isaiah 40:31).

Something in us longs to be raised up, to be gloriously alive. And this feeling comes straight out of taking our God-given gifts and passions to the "next level" and giving God all the glory. Just like mom said.

Of course, it's easier said than done.

Haiti

Not long ago I traveled to Haiti to speak at a Women's Leadership conference. Over two hundred women from across Haiti gathered to learn more about God's calling on their lives.

It was exciting, especially since when we started the ministry, ***NancyHicksLive*** in January 2016, I had prayed, "God, I want to be a part of the 'global Hallelujah!'" The trip to Haiti felt like a wonderful first step.

From seminary and by being part of a missions-minded church, I knew that God is moving in the nations like never before in history. Africa, Latin America, Asia, the Majority World Church (everywhere outside the west) is seeing people coming to faith in Jesus Christ by the hundreds of thousands daily. Coming to Life!

So I'd pray, "God, please get me to the nations." The nations need leaders, Bible teachers, and preachers to handle the large number of people coming to faith. So I was thrilled to be invited to Haiti. But it wasn't what I expected—starting with our first evening of worshiping together.

Where's the Worship?

I love to worship. I'm first and foremost a worshipper. God doesn't make you a singer who deeply loves Him, and not give you a song in your heart primarily for Him. That's worship. But that first evening, I was surprised.

Huh, we're singing all Hillsong worship music.

Nothing wrong with that, of course. I love Hillsong! But I noticed there were no Haitian worship choruses. No "heart language" music. In fact, between the choice of music and style of worship, there was little cultural distinction from my non-denominational church just outside Philadelphia.

Seemed weird to me.

While in Haiti, I spent quite a bit of time with missionaries. I met with humble, beautiful people of God who'd devoted their lives to the Gospel in Haiti. But many of them were on the brink of burnout. One missionary woman I had just met cried out to me one evening, "Nancy, the church is dead here! Lifeless."

I saw it for myself just before the worship service one Sunday morning. I sat in an adult Bible class. Around the small room were approximately twenty people, a mixture of white missionaries and Haitians. The missionary woman who opened the Scriptures scowled. She "explained" the Scriptures with a joyless face. Judgment was laced throughout her lesson. At one point I heard her say, "Do not marry a pretty lady. They're nothing but trouble."

Avoiding her steely stare, I gazed over to my left across the room. Two men sat side-by-side: one white missionary, hunched over, eyes barely open, elbow on knee, fist supporting his would-be hanging head. Right beside him sat a Haitian man. Mirror image.

My heart sank.

It was a snapshot of us exporting our western apathy and lethargy to the nations. *Lord, why?* I asked. *Why are you showing me this? Where's the amazing news about your Church that I've been hearing of?*

Bad News

Today we see two extremes in the Church. A dichotomy: Alive! Or barely breathing.

The world is suffering, too. Take the refugee crisis. It's not hyperbole. It's a real disaster. I saw a little Syrian girl, displaced from her home, appear on *The Today Show*. She told the watching world, "This is enough! Do something! Help us!" Hosting nations are doing their best, but it's hard. Classrooms are overcrowded. Infectious diseases are rampant. It's a world crisis.

Then there're the crises closer to home. If I write "pink ribbon," you know exactly what I mean. Chances are you or someone you love has crossed paths with cancer. Racism, inequality for women, the harsh treatment of the environment, and a sundry of divisions plague us. The 2016 American presidential election is one case in point.

November 11, 2016, was a monumental moment in time. While working on an early morning show, as one of a room full of QVC on-air talents, I stood watching President Trump's acceptance speech. While waiting to go on air, our eyes were glued to the green room TV, which I can assure you, was not on our usual QVC channel. Social media went mad.

The country was divided. The Church, including godly leaders, some within their own marriages, divided over this last election. Many Facebook users shut down their accounts or temporarily suspended use after the election. Life got more difficult.

It's enough to make you want to burrow in your home. But hang with me. It gets personal.

It Gets Personal

You, like I, have suffered bad news too close for comfort. I get it. I had a father who abused our family and then deserted us—twice—leaving my mom to raise three girls on her own.

In my twenty-nine years of marriage to Cam, I've struggled with serious temptations that could have destroyed our family. I, like you, have sat at the bedside of loved ones and watched them die. I've been utterly undone by sexual abuse slithering right into our family. Betrayal that came out of our own Bible-focused, Christ-honoring church. Like I said, it's enough to make you want to hunker down or throw in the towel.

But there's hope.

I don't know your disappointments, your bad news realities, but here's what I do know: there is Good News. God loves you and calls you to life. God calls to you: Eyes up! Look here! Listen in.

- To you who may be struggling to believe anything good could come from all of this,
- To you who struggle to believe . . . period,
- To you who long to see a sliver of goodness or hope anywhere,
- And to the barely-breathing Church everywhere, the message goes out:

You were meant to live!

God's Calling

The core, overarching calling that emerges from the Genesis 3 scene is not a "then." It's very much a "now." The reverberation of God's call, "Come. Live!" is arguably increasing in intensity.

It doesn't take a trip to Haiti to see how far we've gotten from our meant-to-live calling. I came alive in Christ when I was just a little girl, so I've been in the Church a long time. I grew up in Toronto, Canada, moved to Lincoln, Nebraska, for a couple of years, and have lived in the Philadelphia area since 2002. Every place we've lived, we've looked for the Church. Finding a part of the Church to plug in to has been necessary.

I've traveled and ministered to countless churches. As I've experienced the Church in North America, I often felt that Genesis scene so strongly. We sing songs that say we'll "dance and sing like we're dancing now," while yawning and, Lord knows, barely moving. *Really?* The irony is too thick to stand. It's dishonest. Uninspiring.

But there really is good news.

Glorious Good News

Did you know you're glorious? Did you know that all across Scripture we find a glory on humanity? A life-laden glory.

For instance, the apostle Paul emphasized this in his letter to the Church at Colossae: *"[I] present to you the word of God in its fullness—the mystery that has been hidden for ages and generation but is now disclosed to the Lord's people. To them God has chosen to make known among the Gentiles the glorious riches of this mystery, which is **Christ in you, the hope of glory"** (Colossians 1:25-27, emphasis mine).

Pause. Don't miss that. "The hope of glory."

It's the Gospel. And it's Good News.

The Gospel

Track humanity's glory throughout the Gospel, aka the Good News. Four main points capture the overarching meta-narrative of the Scripture:

1. Creation: Humanity was created to be in relationship with God. Alive. Glorious creatures. Crowned with glory and honor and made just a little lower than the angels (Genesis 1:27, 31, 2:7; Psalm 8:5; Hebrews 2:7).

2. Fall: A definite fall from our original glory. Humanity is separated from God. Humanity's glory is veiled and yet, we still bear His image (Genesis 1:27, 3).

3. Jesus: God's solution to the separation. In Christ we are made glorious once more (Colossians 1:27; Romans 8:29; Hebrews 12:1, 2).

4. Restoration: When Jesus returns to establish His kingdom, *"on earth as it is in heaven,"* humanity will be fully glorified (2 Thessalonians 1:12; 2 Peter 3:13; Revelation. 21:1).

Do you see it? Three out of the four—the majority of the Gospel—is your glory, for God and from God, through God and to God.

But in light of the rough state of affairs, there's a strong possibility you're not exactly experiencing this from where you sit. Look around. How many

Christians do you look at and say, "I want to be like that"?

Four Camps

What I've often experienced in the Church and what I saw again in Haiti, for example, is a focus on the one part of the Gospel story that has to do with our *marred* glory. Our fall. Our fruit-eating fiasco. Fixating on sin is camping out in the bad news.

Here are four examples of what I'm seeing in the Church (at least in North America) today:

1. The Untapped Camp: This camp says, "We're doomed. We're nothing. We bring nothing good to the picture. Our hearts are wicked and deceitful. We're dust. Just a grain of sand on the beach, so what do you expect?"

2. The Truth Protector Camp: This camp agrees with the first camp, but takes it a step further—into works. Truth Protectors can have a very academic approach to God and the Scriptures. Out of protection for the Church and Scripture, they can have sharp responses to the other camps. They're sort of like Christian police. "I'm guarding and watching."

3. The Keepin' It Real Camp: This group of campers reacts to the Truth Protectors. They're comfortable with the messy state of life. They're proud to say, "I'm a mess. Sure, I make bad decisions." Obedience to Christ is a nice suggestion, they insist, just not realistic. "But He loves me and at least I'm honest." The crazy state of the world, and of the Church has this camp often messaging, "Let's just get along. Live and let live."

4. The #Blessed Camp: They look at all the above and say, "You guys are nuts! Don't you know the Gospel? Jesus died to give us everything. Everything!" They insist, "Come to Jesus and your life will be fabulous. YOU will be fabulous." It's the American Dream on steroids—in Jesus name.

All four groups are reacting to or avoiding each other entirely. They're slopping around in the bad news. #Blessed reacts to Untapped and Truth Protectors or vice versa. Keepin' It Reals react to Truth Protectors and vice versa. Each is reacting to the other, but not actually responding to God's core call: Life!

In fact, there's a bit of truth in all of them, isn't there? And each of us has leanings toward one or more of these camps. Some reasons we're aware of, others we're not. But in the end, they're all distortions of the Gospel.

The Tensions

But we are glorious beings created and longing for Life.

My mom's constant reminder, "Give the glory to God" is bang on. But what does it actually mean? How do we do that?

'Cause we want to believe it. Really. We do. But like much of Scripture, we live in paradoxes. Seeming contradictions. On one hand the Scriptures are teeming with: *"You are glorious."* At the same time we're warned: *"God will not share his glory with another"* (Isaiah 42:8). But it seems He does, doesn't it?

We live in the center of that biblical tension.

You may already be thinking: *These are such lofty ideas.* And skepticism sets in. Or instead you're thinking: *Careful. You're getting dangerously close to stealing God's glory.* And soon on the heels of such Good News, we pull back. Fear and caution rise in us. Within short order, the desire and life that comes, dissipates. Snatched from our hopeful clutches.

We then quickly take our positions in our camps and get back to sloshing around in the bad news. We scrap with the world and those we differ from in the Church. We avoid each other. We avoid the grand idea of living in a God-ordained glory.

Or.

We can believe God and join Him.

Through this book, I aim to simply present a Scripture-based depiction of God's glory in you, in His Church, 'cause right now you may not be seeing it. If you care at all, you could get easily dismayed. But let's not be dismayed. The Good News of life that Jesus came to bring is a present-day reality. It's Good News that matches the hour!

Into the reams of bad news, God will show up. He always has. His glory is unstoppable.

Join Him there.

CHAPTER 4

The Untapped

"For he knows how we are formed, he remembers that we are dust." Psalm 103:14

Imagine showing up at Disney World and then discovering two problems: They're at full capacity that day, and you can't afford the entrance fee. But you're with a friend who has clout and gets you in, *and* pays your way. Great!

Now imagine going from exhibit to exhibit, ride to ride, all day long saying, "This is too good. I shouldn't. This is too nice. I can't. I mean, I shouldn't even be here." And on and on you go.

At some point your friend with the clout may look at you and say, "You know what would make me happy and really show gratitude? Enjoy the park! Let's have fun! Get on the roller coaster. Zip down the water slides! Thank me from that place."

Who Are the Untapped?

This scenario gives us a good picture of the Untapped, our first camp of Christians. Often those in this camp have internal restrictions. Freedom has been squelched, doused by cold water. They've internalized the message, "Don't have too much fun. Don't be colorful. Don't attract attention. Do you know what you are? Dust. Just a grain of sand on the beach."

Sadly, for many this theology has been deeply ingrained. Some have grown up hearing or deciding for themselves as life has unfolded, "lower your expectations. Don't ask, don't hope."

There are many high-functioning Untapped. They're accomplished and active. They have families, hold down great jobs, and are leaders.

To illustrate: One very accomplished business executive told me, "I keep wondering if someone's going to spot me one day and shout, 'IMPOSTER!'"

Another academic scholar and senior leader in the church shared, "I struggle to walk in a room because I fear finding out I'm not supposed to be there. I'm not invited. What if they say, 'Who let her in?'"

Well-educated, successful followers of Jesus struggle with this lowly mentality. Though in many ways they've overcome, inwardly they fight the needling and nagging thought, *You're one wrong move away from being found out and kicked out.*

Some of these Untapped get overlooked easily because they defer to others. They don't feel right speaking up. Asking for what they'd like seems presumptuous, like a demand. Often these Untapped stand by and let others run the show.

Others of the Untapped are on a different level. I've heard some say without a hint of sarcasm, things like:

- What do I know?
- I knew *you* were somebody, I could just tell.
- Everybody loves *you*. Everyone wants to be with you. (The subtext? "Nobody wants to be with me.")

They let others finish their sentences, sometimes getting cut off midstream. They frequently let others carry the conversation or even speak for them, while they listen quietly.

The Untapped go about quietly challenging or cautioning anything that faintly detects beauty or glory. They quietly sow seeds of lowliness in themselves and others.

Why Untapped?

People come to the Untapped camp honestly. Good intentions have paved the way to this sort of thinking and behaving. Basically it boils down to theology—a view of God and how we relate to Him. Two key factors have influenced this theology.

Scripture

There are passages in Scripture that have been used to support the idea that humans are unworthy:

- *"The heart is deceitful above all things and beyond cure. Who can understand it?"* (Jeremiah 17:9).
- *"The LORD saw how great the wickedness of the human race had become on the earth, and that every inclination of the thoughts of the human heart was only evil all the time..."* (Genesis 6:5).
- *"There is no one righteous, not even one; there is no one who understands; there is no one who seeks God. All have turned away, they have together become worthless; there is no one who does good, not even one"* (Romans 3:10-12).

The Untapped read these passages and think: "Yep. This is what we see each day on the news. Heck, it's what I see in my family. Have you met my cousin?" The Untapped take it in, and over and over have their hypothesis confirmed: *We're a mess. Full of depravity. Small and meaningless. Frankly, Jesus can't come soon enough for me.*

These biblical truths, though incomplete, then get expressed in song.

Music

"When you sing, you pray twice," said the great Church father, Augustine of Hippo.[3] Prayer and music are a dynamo combo and carry tremendous power. Power on our emotions, minds, bodies, souls—and therefore they exert power over our worship and whole life experience. From the guts of our being, our breath carries the voice of the Church.

But it goes both ways: positive and negative. The great music of the centuries-old Church has lyrics we can point to that support the Untapped mentality:

"Alas! and Did My Savior Bleed"

Alas! and did my Savior bleed?

And did my Sovereign die?

Would He devote that sacred head

For such a worm as I?[4]

"Amazing Grace"

Amazing grace! How sweet the sound,

That saved a wretch like me!

I once was lost, but now am found,

Was blind, but now I see.[5]

Of course I'm not disputing the tremendous merit in these lyrics. As with many hymns, they unpack a sound theology. There's truth there, but it's woefully incomplete. And often, through a whole song like "Amazing Grace" which does include a complete view of the gospel, the Untapped latch onto one lyric: *That saved a wretch like me.* For some, that one line underscores and confirms a life-long suspicion or outright belief: *I'm a wretch.*

But don't blame John Newton! It's the context that's skewed things— our view of our wretchedness is out of proportion. As in prayer, if our main focus in the overall corporate worship experience is on our unworthiness and not on Christ's resurrection power and life, it will be an issue.

I love our church. The church's leadership takes the gospel, the authority of Scripture, and Christ's reign very seriously. Yet a few years ago, I noticed a stream of Sundays where a combination of the overall tone (including visuals, pacing, and low energy in prayer and music) draped the sanctuary in Gethsemane and Golgotha. (And no, it wasn't Lent or Good Friday.) I could barely keep my hand from popping up to say, "Hold on. Aren't we missing something?"

Part of why we gather as a community is to celebrate God's glory. His beauty. His goodness. I found myself actually becoming fatigued and frustrated in hearing such a constant and heavy dose of bad news with too little lift to balance it out.

This self-flagellating "worship" actually works well for some Untapped. It confirms what feels right to them. But for those who fight the insidious feeling of guilt, condemnation, or those God has pulled out of horrific pasts and rough circumstances, it's tough. We know where we've been, and we're not there anymore. We're His beloved! His Bride. And experientially we really know it! To us, *not* celebrating the resurrection—on any given Sunday—feels really off.

Though founded in Scripture and reiterated in Church music, the issue is an inordinate retelling of the ugly story. It's an over-emphasis of either who we "are" (sinners saved by grace) or what we've "done" (messed up again).

Of course I know some have never actually grasped the depth of their need of a Savior. Most definitely it's what keeps many people who don't know Christ from seeing their need of Him, but they're likely in a different camp. Those of you, dear Untapped, who have low self-esteem and hide, could use a triple dose of the *Good* news.

Tapped

Jesus went about tapping people all the time.

One day He approached a pool near the Sheep Gate, or Bethesda. Watch what happened when he approached the disabled: *"Here a great number of disabled people used to lie—the blind, the lame, the paralyzed. One who was there had been an invalid for thirty-eight years. When Jesus saw him lying there and learned that he had been in this condition for a long time, he asked him, 'Do you want to get well?'"* (John 5:3-6).

I love that Jesus asked, "Do you want to get well?" On the face of it, it seems an absurd question. Who wouldn't want to be well? Actually, lots of people. "Don't mess up my routine, Jesus. Don't expect too much. I've got a good thing going." You know people like this, right?

But that was not the attitude of the man at Bethesda. He replied, "*I have no one to help me into the pool . . . While I am trying to get in, someone else goes down ahead of me*" (John 5:7). This previously Untapped man might have blamed everybody else. Making excuses. Choosing to exert feeble, if any effort.

Thankfully, that wasn't his attitude. He had a desire to be well, to rise up. And at Christ's command, he did.

Then Jesus said to him, "*Get up! Pick up your mat and walk. At once the man was cured; he picked up his mat and walked*" (John 5:8, 9).

This passage brings up other groups of the Untapped—those sidelined or underutilized. In this Gospel passage, Jesus tapped a crippled man. Literally crippled. The Body of Christ would be wise to tap the tremendous giftings of believers who are physically and mentally challenged. Bent. Disfigured. Lame. Differently-abled. Asperger's. Down Syndrome. And so forth. All potentially Untapped.

Difference around race, socio-economic level and gender, to name a few, can leave all sorts of people Untapped. And this is so contrary to the Gospel (Matthew 11:28).

For others, some "you're-not-so-special" messaging has come out of shame around personal or family failures. Not physically challenged, but challenged just the same. Many Untapped have experienced divorce, sexual shame, or children who cause them deep sadness.

These Untapped are longing for someone to "tap" them. They long for the Church to see their worth. Some have dismissed themselves by their own sense of inadequacy, or out of their experience of being sidelined. But they're not the only ones.

"Why Would I Go There?"

Philip Yancey tells a story that illustrates.

"A prostitute came to me in wretched straights, homeless, sick, unable to buy food for her two-year-old daughter. Through sobs and tears, she told me she had been renting out her daughter—two years old!—to men interested in kinky sex. She made more renting out her daughter for an hour than she could earn on her own in a night. She had to do it, she said, to support her own drug habit. I could hardly bear hearing her sordid story. For one thing, it made me legally liable—I'm required to report cases of child abuse. I had no idea what to say to this woman. At last I asked if she had ever thought of going to a church for help. I will never forget the look of pure, naïve shock that crossed her face.

"Church?" she cried. "Why would I ever go there? I was already feeling terrible about myself. They'd just make me feel worse."[6]

Yancey's friend clearly needed the Gospel. But for all we know, she could have grown up in the Church. She could have gone to Sunday School and Vacation Bible School. Whatever her experience of the church, it wasn't positive.

Maybe that's how you feel. Maybe prostitution, drug abuse, and sex-trafficking aren't your story, but the feeling of shame from failure or "not quite keeping up" still looms large.

Women

The latest statistics about Christian women in North America are that they're leaving the Church: "Up from the last decade, 45% of adults are unchurched in the U.S. and that trend shows no indication of slowing. The surprise? Increasing number of women who are part of this cultural shift away from churchgoing . . .

"While just over half of all adult women have gone to church in the past week or past month (19% and 36%, respectively), nearly four in 10 have not been to church in the past six months: 38%" (David Kinnaman, "3 Reasons Why Women Are Leaving the Church").[7]

One reason is that many female Christ-followers feel underutilized in the church.

Women today flood the marketplace. 87% of mothers work. 75% of those working mothers work full-time, and that's up from 37% in 1975

(Founder and President of 4WordWomen's Dianne Paddison, "Working Women Are Leaving the Church. Here's How to Bring Them Back").[8]

In the marketplace, they're educators, scientists, politicians, business owners. But in the church, many are still relegated to women's groups (which often meet at inconvenient times for working women) or ministering to children.

While these are vital areas of ministry, for many women today, being told "these are your options" diminishes their opportunity for impact. They're the Untapped.

Not only are women untapped in the west, but around the world.

The Global Woman

In the early stages of my ministry, God has allowed me to minister in Haiti, the Philippines, Albania, and East Asia. My goal, by the grace of God, is to raise up women around the globe. Culturally, women are still marginalized and oppressed in much of the world. But they're often the workhorses in the church! Still, in most cases, most of the biblical and leadership training goes to the men.

Please hear me: I do not begrudge men being raised up, trained, and equipped. Not in the least. Many fabulous men, including pastors and leaders work tirelessly for the kingdom of God. But, hello! Women are running hard after God and moving out like wildfire! Lack of resources (of every kind) can leave an entire half of the Body of Christ, in some way Untapped.

Albania

One woman stands out in my mind. In Northern Albania, I met and served a woman who works as a pastor in two churches (an hour apart) and weekly leads three Bible classes in one of those churches and two in the other. *Weekly.*

So with very little money, (her husband is a farmer, with little to no opportunity to make a living in the dry, unfriendly terrain of Albania), she drives between the two churches working with what she's got. She has little training to pastor or teach the Scriptures. This is common in the Majority World Church even among men, but it's especially common among women.

As a minister of the Gospel, one of my main goals is to ignite a passion for Christ, by the power of the Holy Spirit, in women across the globe. They're not the Untapped from an ingrained theology. Their life experience has demanded they lower their expectations. Many haven't had the training or equipping. Still they work hard knowing they're tapped by God. Perhaps they simply need the Church to get behind that tapping!

But, let's be real, it's not just Christians. Ask any woman in a career that's historically been occupied by men—business, politics, science, film—and they'll tell you, this is not unique to the Church. But I believe the Church should be leading the way toward change.

These are examples of the Untapped. Camping out, for whatever the reason, in thought or practice, in bad news.

Some have "solved" this issue by avoiding the Church:

"I get my church by watching it on TV," one woman told me.

"I pull up podcasts and videos anytime I like," say others.

The idea of joining a faith community isn't so appealing.

"They're not going to miss me," they think.

"I'm just busy."

"Sunday's the only day I really get to relax."

"Been there. Done that."

Whether it's our boundaries or their own, we would do well to at least begin to recognize that this Untapped camp is full of people ready for some Good News.

Strengths

And of course there are tremendous strengths they bring to the picture.

Listening

The Untapped have well-honed strengths. Quietly listening is one. The Untapped have often spent a lot of time in churches that have graduate degrees in guilt and shame.

They've chosen to get by through listening. They're not passive. They're *really* listening.

Those of us who are verbal and demonstrative would do well to take a page from the Untapped. In fact, those of us who lean toward other camps would do well to make a little room for the Untapped. Give them some space to open up and spread their wings or lean in and pay attention.

But sadly, often the idea that someone would lean in and pay attention to them can be uncomfortable. They think: *It's not my turn. Which is ironic, because they have remarkable depth to share.*

Wisdom

"Wise (wo)men speak because they have something to say; Fools because they have to say something." —Plato

Because the Untapped spend time listening well, they are often a reservoir of wisdom. The Untapped often possess insight into situations and people that's off the charts!

Take the courageous, civil rights activist Rosa Parks:

"I was riding the bus home from work. A white man got on, and the driver looked our way and said, 'Let me have those seats.' It did not seem proper, particularly for a woman to give her seat to a man. All the passengers paid ten cents, just as he did. When more whites boarded the bus, the driver, J.P. Blake ordered the blacks in the fifth row, the first of the colored section (the row I was sitting in), to move to the rear.

"At first none of us moved. 'Y'all better make it light on yourselves and let me have those seats,' Blake said.

"Then three of the blacks in my row got up, but I stayed in my seat and slid closer to the window. I do not remember being frightened. But I sure did not believe I would 'make it light' on myself by standing up. Our mistreatment was just not right, and I was tired of it."[9]

Wisdom is often lived out in quieter ways. Rosa Parks stood against evil and helped define history.

Humility

Another beautiful strength of the Untapped is humility. And who would challenge the idea that this is a necessary characteristic in a Christ follower?

- *"Do nothing out of selfish ambition or vain conceit. Rather, in humility value others above yourselves"* (Philippians 2:3).
- *"Live in harmony with one another. Do not be proud, but be willing to associate with people of low position. Do not be conceited"* (Romans 12:16).
- *"Sitting down, Jesus called the Twelve and said, 'Anyone who wants to be first must be the very last, and the servant of all'"* (Mark 9:35).

These, among a whole host of other verses, draw on the humility of Jesus, the humility that led Him to earth, then to a cross (Philippians 2:7, 8).

Postures of humility are often found in this camp. More listening. Considering others above self. Taking less than others (a smaller portion of rice, or none at all, or a parking spot that's *not* closest to the entrance). Regardless of whether or not this comes from genuine humility, the desire and posture of humility is often there. This goes a long way in a culture and time that rejects humility.

"Be number one!"

"Go big or go home."

"Compete, compete, compete."

And our Untapped sisters notice. They dig deeper. Their internal pendulum swings to counter the apparent lack of humility.

From high-functioning to marginalized, the Untapped experience low-grade to extreme feelings of unworthiness that diminish God's call to life.

Do you relate?

Think about your church: who's in your congregation, your Bible study or small group? Knowing your audience matters. If you're a church leader and have any influence on your services, just take a month-long look at the majority of messaging—content, tone, atmosphere, body language—and see if you have, deliberately or inadvertently, camped out on the bad news. Have you focused on "unworthiness," minimizing God's call to life and glory?

The Truth Protectors sometimes help reinforce the sense of unworthiness in the Untapped. We'll take a look at this profile next.

••●●●●••

The Untapped

The Untapped can be characterized by:

- Having chronic feelings of unworthiness.
- Having depressive, negative thoughts (though not necessarily clinically depressed).
- Focusing on death, dying, smallness, wretchedness

They have thoughts like, or even express:

- What do I know?
- I knew *you* were somebody, I could just tell.
- Everybody loves *you*. Everyone wants to be with you. (But not me.)

Questions:

1. Does any of this sound familiar? Do you know the Untapped?
2. What other group(s) of people would you add to the Untapped list?
3. Do you identify with any of the specific positive or negative characteristics of the Untapped?
4. Which Untapped (disabled, African-American, Latino, women, etc.) do you most want to advocate for? Why?
5. If you consider yourself to be one of the Untapped, how could someone encourage you to allow yourself to be Tapped?

••●●●●••

CHAPTER 5

Truth Protectors

"[We] can't be always defending the truth; there must be a time to feed on it."
—*C.S. Lewis, Reflections of the Psalms*[10]

Jackson's Point

S ummers at Jackson's Point Camp hold a thousand memories for me. Like the Baptists and Methodists, The Salvation Army denomination has conference centers and camps all around the world. A fifteen-year-old female Salvationist who wanted to spend the summer at Jackson's Point and earn some money had one option: get hired as a waitress.

So I did. I packed up my stuff and moved up to the lake for the summer.

I worked diligently serving and clearing tables for the officers (Army-speak for pastors) who vacationed at the conference center. Most nights, after racing around all day, the other waitstaff (the girls) and chore boys (the fifteen-year-old guys) would hang out and maybe watch a movie, but by the end of the day, we were beat. I'd often hunker down in my dorm room and spend some time with God.

I took my relationship with God very seriously, even at fifteen. At that point, I'd already been ministering in music for a few years. I wasn't messing around.

One night, midway through the summer, I was lying on my bed reading my Bible, but felt pulled. A group of kids invited me into town. I usually steered clear of that particular group because they were the "bad" kids. The ones doing stuff that any "serious" Salvationist knew not to do. They knew *I knew* who they were, and they knew I was a "serious" Salvationist. But that night, someone invited me to town.

"Darn it, I'm tired of being a good girl. I want to have some fun."

I closed my Bible, jumped in the car and headed with them to Rosa's Pizza.

So this is what they do at Rosa's, I thought. There I sat, laughing, acting like a hot shot and . . . smoking.

I felt "in." Cool. Like a bad girl.

The next day was Saturday and we had some time off. I went out in a canoe with a couple of girls, way, way out on the lake so we could smoke again. Twice in two days.

That night we had staff devotions. We all gathered around the fireplace in the lounge.

"It's the midway point of our summer," our leader said. "You'll be heading home in a few weeks, back to the world where it's hard to walk with Jesus. It won't be safe like it is here. You'll have to take a stand against all the traps that come your way."

I thought, *Are you kidding me? I do fine with people who don't know Jesus. I know how to love and follow Him there. I know how to stand my ground! HERE is where I let down my guard—with Christians. Now look, I'm smoking!*

I felt awful. I'd been so careful to be good. And I really did love God.

Our leader invited anyone who wanted to pray out loud about returning to "the world" to go ahead.

So I did.

"God, I'm so sorry. I've fallen. I've sinned against you," I confessed out loud to the room full of teenage staff and our leaders. And I meant every word of it. (And I'm sure there was a bit of, "And God, thank you for pulling me out and now exposing the truth about THIS group of so-called 'Christians!'")

The kids who'd introduced me to this life of debauchery tugged at my pant leg, whacked my ankle, and shushed me. "Sit down. Shut up." But I just kept praying and blowing our cover.

Afterward, I called my mom and asked her to make the ninety-minute drive from Toronto up to Jackson's. I told her I had something hard to tell her. She arrived the next morning and we walked along the paths of the camp. She listened as I poured out my heart about my caving into corruption.

"Oh, honey. I thought you were going to tell me you were pregnant or something."

"Mom! This is bad! I've fallen. I'm a hypocrite!" I cried.

At the end of the summer, I sat down with our corps officer (church pastor), Major Skipper, to tell him my shameful story.

"I'd understand if you'd like me to step out of ministry. I probably shouldn't wear the Salvation Army uniform anymore either."

Major Skipper was wise. "Nancy, I think you've punished yourself enough."

If truth be told, I'm a recovering Truth Protector.

Who Are the Truth Protectors?

"The only thing necessary for the triumph of evil is that good [people] do nothing," said Edmund Burke. Truth Protectors agree with him and in reply say, "Not on my watch. I will not allow evil!"

Truth Protectors protect "truth." They have the answers. They're teachers. In fact, Truth Protectors can make everything a "teachable moment." They want to solve problems you didn't even know you had. If you've ever had a moment when a friend told you the "truth" when all you needed was to vent, or a shoulder to cry on, or a light-hearted night out, you've met a Truth Protector.

Truth Protectors check everything in our conversations, our hymns, our versions of Scripture, and even how we pray against their version of doctrinal purity. Truth Protectors raise an eyebrow to associations with certain denom-inations, then make assessments: right or wrong. In or out.

And I must confess, *I've* done that . . . can *still* do that. Sometimes to the people I love most.

For some, especially those steeped in the "teaching type" church tradi-tions, they can impressively dispense Scripture, ever ready with a verse for any situation.

See if you recognize these scenarios:

Megan: "I feel so lonely. Dave's always travelling."
Truth Protector: "God is with you. He'll never leave you."

Jenn: "I don't know where my confidence has gone. It's like I can't do anything."
Truth Protector: "Remember, 'I can do all things through Christ who strengthens me.'"

John: "I'm really pretty good at this. Look, I'm doing it!"
Truth Protector: "Be careful. Pride goes before a fall."

Do you know people like this? When needed, they've got the goods. They've got the verse. If they're not giving you the goods, they're thinking it. Oh, trust me they're thinking it. It's right at the front of their mind and often the very tip of their tongue. If not in check, it can be annoying.

I once loaned what I considered a great novel to a friend. She returned it with questions, arrows, underlining and cautions written throughout. She either a.) thought this would somehow get to the author, b.) needed to vent or c.) was cautioning me, her younger friend who'd bought the book in the first place.

She felt compelled to be vigilant. She couldn't just enjoy the book.

Sadly, I've seen Truth Protectors bashing and doing the "en garde!" routine on social media. Back and forth. Poking and prodding theology then pronouncing authors, leaders, and Bible teachers, "heretical!" It's *exhausting*. It may be invigorating for them, but it can be exhausting for those around them.

These heresy hunters may point out the faults in others as a way of diverting attention from dealing with their own issues. But for many, in all that judging, critiquing, guarding, and correcting, naturally a bit of paranoia can creep in. The Truth Protector begins to think: *If I'm thinking this way, others are probably thinking this of me.*

Truth Protectors are very concerned about what people think of them. Why? Because they're "good." They play by the rules. And they need to be seen that way.

The Elder Brother

The quintessential Truth Protectors are the elder brother in the parable of the prodigal son. Jesus told this parable to a group of Pharisees (the very serious, scripturally-literate Yahweh followers of the day), while a group of "sinners" were listening in.

You'll remember in the parable, the elder brother was ticked off that the younger brother got such a fantastic reception when he returned from his life of debauchery.

"The older brother became angry and refused to go in. So his father went out and pleaded with him. But he answered his father, 'Look! All these years I've been slaving for you and never disobeyed your orders. Yet you never gave me even a young goat so I could celebrate with my friends. But when this son of yours who has squandered your property with prostitutes comes home, you kill the fattened calf for him!'" (Luke 15:28-30).

The words that immediately come to me when I read that passage are: that's not fair! Truth Protectors like things to be fair. They watch and work for fairness, especially when it's in their favor. And why shouldn't it be? They play by the rules. But when things aren't fair and don't go their way, they're often angry.

And as in the case of the elder brother, Truth Protectors harbor secret pride.

False Humility

Truth Protectors often strike a *posture of humility* because they know humility is a virtue, not because they genuinely are humble.

It's what the apostle Paul warns against in Colossians when he speaks of "false humility" (Colossians 2:23).

False humility lacks grace. It's the refusal of a compliment with the insistent, "It's all God. I bring nothing to the table. Glory to God alone!"

Of course, true humility is very much the Gospel. True humility exudes an honest assessment of self. True humility is free to genuinely applaud another, even another whose gift-set or lifestyle are similar to your own. The truly humble don't become architects of their own praise.

Image management (what are people thinking of me or those I care about?) can leave Truth Protectors feeling pretty insecure. Insecurity is a genuine struggle for Truth Protectors, much like the Untapped. They may feel profoundly insecure, for example about how God is getting portrayed. They feel obliged to be God's P.R. agents, when in fact God doesn't really need one. Truth Protectors are on the offense for God and His Truth. And for good reason.

Truth Matters

It's a crazy world. In Western Culture, truth is up for grabs.

"This is my truth." Sound familiar? The idea is that how you experience something, based on your history, environment, personality, etc. forms a certain "reality" or truth unlike anyone else's. "I'm not happy in this marriage," may very well be your "truth." Your next-door neighbor may say the same thing. "I'm also not happy in my marriage," but her experience is different in myriad ways. In both cases "truth" is what you see of your experience today, but it's only a sliver of the total reality.

The troubling part is that personal experience is clouding genuine, immovable truth.

Pilate's Problem

In the first century, the political leader, Pontius Pilate scoffed, "what is truth?" while washing his hands of the outcome of Jesus. Jesus Christ was crucified, in part, by Pontius Pilate's avoidance of the issue of whether Jesus or another prisoner would be released. A custom implemented to gain favor with the masses.

Pilate refused to take a stand to release Jesus in order to avoid upsetting the Jews, risking a riot. He dodged the issue (Mark 15). Thus he sent Jesus to his death, though Jesus claimed all the way to that death, *"I am the Way, the Truth, and the Life"* (John 14:6). Pilate's ambiguity about the truth killed Jesus (aka Truth). The irony is dense.

Truth Protectors fear such uncertainty.

Anything Goes

Several hundred years before Jesus came in the flesh, God's people were also in a time of "anything goes." Scripture uses a great phrase for that which I believe can be applied to our own era: *"In those days Israel had no king; all the people did **whatever seemed right in their own eyes**"* (Judges 21:25, emphasis mine).

We live in a time where people do what seems *right in their own eyes*.

- "If my eight-year-old son says he's always wanted to be a girl, that's his truth."
- "If I'm single and want to have sex, why not? It's unreasonable to wait for a husband who might never show up."

Truth Protectors think and pray and sometimes agonize over such issues. Sometimes it's because they're the ones having to make the decisions that affect all sorts of people in a congregation. Truth Protectors are often leaders.

The apostle John writes to warn the children of God in the first century: *"Dear friends, do not believe every spirit, but test the spirits to see whether they are from God, because many false prophets have gone out into the world"* (1 John 4:1).

Truth Protectors don't pull these things out of thin air. They're real. As leaders, they're often the gatekeepers and protectors.

Unrighteousness motivates Truth Protectors. They're also motivated by a lack of control and fear—fear of losing ground, fear of losing impact. Such conditions cause them to tighten their grip.

Perfectionism

The intentions of Truth Protectors are not bad, they're just sometimes skewed. In their pursuit of righteousness, they've veered into paralyzing perfectionism.

When you seek perfection, you can lose the joy and celebration. You can't celebrate and live life to the full when you're always on the offense. Like a singer who sings technically well, can sight-read, or even has perfect pitch, but gets preoccupied with particulars. Such a singer can't make music that brings shivers down your spine or makes you purr like a kitten. The mechanics sometimes get in the way.

Almost Perfect

Once I was in a dictation class in the music program at the University of Toronto.

One student was impressive! She could listen to successions of chords and identify each and every note in the progression. We all knew she was phenomenal at this exercise. She had perfect pitch.

In the final exam, we all sat at our desks while the professor played the chord progressions and we wrote down each note we heard. We all hoped to just pass, never mind get perfect scores.

My classmate looked perplexed at one point during the exam. The professor noticed. If she was perplexed, what hope did the rest of us have?

He played the chord progression again. She still looked confused. She finally broke protocol and spoke up, "Why is there an F# in this chord? There shouldn't be. It's wrong."

"There isn't," the professor responded.

"Yes, there is," she asserted.

We all sat silently wondering who was right.

Then in our silence, a jackhammer working beyond the windows on the sidewalk below played that perfect F# that was messing with her world! Even when we try for perfection, the world gets in the way and we drive ourselves crazy.

Jesus told the Truth Protectors of the day, "You diligently study the Scriptures because you think that by them you possess eternal life. These are the Scriptures that point to me and yet you refuse to come to me and live" (John 5:39).

In other words, "You're stuck. You're all caught up. You're exhausted and lifeless. But you don't have to be."

Our weaknesses are often the flip side of our strengths. And of course Truth Protectors can be highly effective.

Strengths of Truth Protectors

We've all been on the receiving end of Truth Protectors acting in their strengths. They've had the right thought, verse, or guidance at just the right time. Here are a few strengths:

They Lead

Truth Protectors refuse to let chaos reign. When a situation calls for action, they're on it! Ever-watchful for signs that their commitment to Truth is needed.

They're Protective

Truth Protectors protect. They're vigilant and active, keeping watch and working for good.

They take seriously the work of God and take responsibility of protecting the flock. And good thing!

They're Passionate

When Truth Protectors are exemplifying their strengths from a healthy place, they're on it! The Truth Protector is summed up in this quote from one of my heroes of the faith, Evangeline Booth:

"If a woman loves, she worships.

If she champions a cause, she'll fight for it.

If she gives, she gives all.

If she lives for, she dies for."

That's a picture of an honest-to-goodness, powerhouse Truth Protector in all her glory!

Teaching Type

Truth Protectors often have a gift for discipling and teaching. Often, even when they're not saying a word, their lives are teaching us. They are our elders, pastors, Bible teachers, and mentors. Because they're up front, we get the idea that this is what it looks like to live an exemplary Christian life. We feel they're our poster-child: "Be like her!"

In many ways this is a wonderful gift to the Body of Christ.

--------------- •·•●●●•·· ---------------

Truth Protectors

Truth Protectors can be characterized by:

- Having high integrity.
- Commitment to justice and righteousness.
- Valuing knowledge.
- Exhibiting leadership qualities.
- Hard on self and others. Critical, correcting.

- Lack of genuine joy.
- Finding it difficult to relax.

They may have thoughts like, or even express:

- "Careful, you're dangerously close to . . ."
- "The Bible says . . ." as a frequent precursor to a correction.
- "They weren't quite accurate about . . ."

Questions:

1. Does any of this sound familiar? Do you know any Truth Protectors?

2. When you've experienced Truth Protectors in your home, church, the workplace, online, on the street corner, how have they moved you toward and/or away from life?

3. If this sounds like you, write a few words or sentences expressing your feelings and/or thoughts on this type.

4. If you have unintentionally hurt someone by being a Truth Protector, how might you have been able to be more compassionate?

CHAPTER 6

Keepin' It Reals

"Cheap grace is grace without discipleship." —Dietrich Bonhoeffer[11]

I love real. I love honest. Candor and transparency are high values for me. Imagine sitting down and poring over a menu at a lovely new café, finally deciding on the elegantly described "fromage grille and pomme frites" only to be served a grilled cheese and French fries. I think we all, at some level, long for authenticity and "keepin' it real."

So don't be confused by what I've named this camp of Christians. One of their strengths is that they're honest. They're real. We love them for it.

Though honesty and transparency are desperately needed virtues, the Keepin' It Reals almost celebrate the choices that lead to the messy state of their lives.

"All have sinned and fall short of the glory of God," is often translated by the Keepin' It Reals into, "Why even try?"

Sin as a Four-Letter Word

In fact, the word "sin" is offensive to Keepin' It Reals. *Isn't that a bit judgmental? A bit outdated and harsh?* they think.

Author David Brooks describes the attitude toward sin today. He notes that we've replaced that dirty, little word with other words like "mistake" and "weakness."

"When modern culture tries to replace sin with ideas like error or insensitivity, or tries to banish words like 'virtue,' 'character,' 'evil,' and 'vice' altogether, that doesn't make life any less moral; it just means we have obscured the inescapable moral core of life with shallow language. It just means we think and talk about these choices less clearly, and thus become increasingly blind to the moral stakes of everyday life."[12]

The Keepin' It Reals have decided to settle for moral failure. *Yes, I'm confessing my wrongs, but what I do with that information is my business. I may or may not change.*

Grace

The Keepin' It Real often says, "It's all about grace."

Thank God for grace! Grace, of course, is God's unmerited, undeserved, unearned favor. But the Keepin' It Reals say, "Because I don't have to do anything to earn God's love and acceptance, I'm free to do and be what I please."

The Keepin' It Reals embrace all things in the name of grace, tolerance, and good will to all. "And what's wrong with that?" you may wonder.

Cheap Grace

Dietrich Bonhoeffer coined the phrase "cheap grace" when extrapolating upon a verse in the apostle Paul's letter to the Romans. *"What shall we say, then? Shall we go on sinning so that grace may increase? By no means!"* (Romans 6:1, 2a).

"Cheap grace is the grace we bestow on ourselves. Cheap grace is the preaching of forgiveness without requiring repentance . . . Cheap grace is grace without discipleship, grace without the cross, grace without Jesus Christ, living and incarnate."[13]

Obedience to God and holiness are lower priorities for the Keepin' It Reals than authenticity. They have a perhaps unconscious attitude that they'll accept Jesus as forgiver and friend. But that's as far as they can commit.

When I share what it means to be a follower of Jesus, I use two descriptors. He's forgiver and leader. It's one thing to say, "I choose Jesus." It's another thing to now say, "Lead on, Jesus. I'll go where you go. I'll do what you do in all things."

CEO God

A few years ago, one of the stylists I worked with at QVC told me her six-year-old son prayed, "Jesus, I want to ask you into my heart, 'cause I don't want to go to hell. But I'm not ready to follow you yet."

We laughed at that. It was so honest and raw, and frankly, I think many Christians live by that mantra, but of course, would never actually utter those words.

The dirty, little secret of many Keepin' It Reals is that living the life with God as CEO is just too much to ask. They've tried and failed. They've read the Scriptures. They know obedience to Christ is not optional. Calling hinges on obedience. Our core calling that we were meant to live will never be realized without it. And they know. So guilt looms.

No Lord

The chapel speaker at a Christian college wrapped up his charge to the students to boldly live for Christ and to obediently go where He led. Challenged, the students filed out of the college chapel.

As the speaker gathered his things, he noticed one young woman sitting in the balcony, long after the others had left. He climbed the stairs and gently approached her.

She was hunched over. Her long hair hung, obscuring her tears.

He spoke kindly. "May I sit with you?" he asked.

"Sure," she whispered.

"Why the tears?"

"I'm graduating soon, and for months, it's been clear that God is calling me to spend my life serving in Guatemala."

"Hmm . . . And you're crying because . . ."

"Because I don't want to. I don't want to leave my family and live in Guatemala."

"I see," he empathized.

Then he pulled out a piece of paper and wrote down two words: No Lord. He handed her the paper.

"I'm going to leave you alone with God. When I return, you will have crossed out one of these words. They can't exist together. Cross out 'Lord' if you won't allow God's leadership in your life. Or cross out 'no' and declare today, and every day after, 'God, you're in charge. You are Lord of this life."

Keepin' It Reals, find the "Lord" part of being a Christian really tough.

In fact, many find it so hard to face Truth Protectors and other "goodies" (many of whom they've been corrected and felt judged by), so they avoid church. "I can get church on podcasts and YouTube. I like the preaching better anyway."

Why Keepin' It Real?

As with all the camps, there are many reasons Christians get stuck there. See if these ring true.

Can't Do This

I have a dear friend who came to believe in Jesus, to her own surprise. Miho struggled for years to figure out how to then live for Him. She roamed from church to church—Catholic, to Southern Baptist, to Pentecostal. The problem wasn't with God. She was sold on Jesus. Her problem was with His people.

There were just too many rules and rituals for this bold, adventurous, uber-creative woman.

She says in her one-woman show, "If that's what Christianity is, I guess I can't be a Christian."[14] It was years before she finally landed in a congregation where she could really grow.

Keepin' It Reals often struggle to find their place in the church family. Sometimes they compare themselves with their Christian sisters and don't feel they measure up. She may determine: *All positions are filled. I'm not needed or wanted.*

They give up: *Forget it. I'm out of here. I love Jesus, but I can't do this thing.* And there's a liberty in facing facts.

Freedom

"It is for freedom that Christ has set us free," (Galatians 5:1) and the championing of this freedom is a focal point for this camp. They rejoice in passages about freedom from "law" (religious rules and regulations).

"But if you are led by the Spirit, you are not under the law" (Galatians 5:18).

Notice what that freedom actually was intended for: *"But do not use your freedom to indulge the flesh; rather, serve one another humbly in love . . . walk by the Spirit, and you will not gratify the desires of the flesh . . . the acts of the flesh are obvious: sexual immorality, impurity and debauchery; idolatry and witchcraft; hatred, discord, jealousy, fits of rage, selfish ambition, orgies, and the like."*

The passage goes on to describe the life under genuine freedom of the Holy Spirit, which leads to fruit revealing genuine growth (Galatians 5:13, 16, 19, 22, 23).

The positive intention, it seems, is to liberate themselves and others from trying too hard and from false selves. They despise the posture of those who say, "I have it all together," or "Isn't Jesus amazing because He's done or given me all this." Because that's not their experience. On a deeper level, for many in the Keepin' It Real camp, life has been a series of rude awakenings, causing them to jolt up in bed at night in a cold, clammy sweat.

Serious Trauma

In some cases, our Keepin' It Reals are actually doing the best they can.

C.S. Lewis provides great insight. Think of someone who suffered serious cruelty since childhood. Now imagine that they do a kind thing, or refrain from being cruel. In God's eyes, she may be doing far more than someone (having grown up without the damage) who dies for a friend.

"That is why Christians are told not to judge," says Lewis. "We see only the results which a man's choices make out of his raw material. But God does not judge him on the raw material at all, but on what he has done with it."[15]

Authority is not a word we really like today. Neither is obedience. They both sound legalistic. Add to that our wariness of abuse of authority everywhere, including the church, from power-hungry hierarchical leaders, authoritarian parents, chauvinistic men, . . . and it's tough. This is what the Keepin' It Reals are reacting to.

"Authority? Obedience? Do you know how dangerous that's been for me?"

Having experienced trauma, many Keepin' It Reals wrestle addictions to substances like drugs and alcohol, or other vices, like lying and sexual cravings.

And as with each camp, they absolutely have their strengths.

Strengths

Honesty

There are a lot of Keepin' It Reals today, simply due to the high value our culture places on authenticity. They snub those they deem "stuck" in the system of society and religiosity. "I'm not perfect like you guys *think* you are. But at least I'm honest."

Honesty isn't relegated to any one socioeconomic group, but I spend a good deal of time ministering in a homeless shelter where there are very few pretenses. Of course there's mental illness and yes, inability to grasp reality, but generally, Christians in the shelter aren't hiding anything. It's obvious: life isn't quite working out the way it seems to be for most everyone else. It's tough to hide behind pretense when you're toothless, your eyes are glazed over, and you're sleeping under a highway.

Some of these men and women who love God and self-identify as Christians can be brutally honest about the horrific upbringings they've endured, and the subsequent choices they've made that have landed them where they are today. Their commitment to honesty is a beautiful thing.

Dependence on God

Keepin' it Reals know they're no match for the devil, who can take them down. They're counting on God. They're counting on Jesus coming through for them. They're not worried about being told that Jesus is their crutch. *Crutch, nothing!* They think, *He's my iron lung.*

Keepin' It Reals know that even if it seems the whole world is against them, God is for them. And even if that belief is constantly challenged, they'll hold onto it. "God *does* love me. God *is* for me." There's a dependence that's noteworthy.

Relational

Maybe foundationally, the Keepin' It Reals, like the rest of us, are scared to death to depend on others—especially since they've often been let down. But the Keepin' It Reals often freely acknowledge their need for others and are unashamed of it.

Compassionate

Keepin' it Reals are acquainted with suffering and, as a result, have great compassion. When there's a bottoming out, and a desperate cry for help, the Keepin' It Reals show up with extraordinary compassion. They're not afraid of mess.

"She who has been forgiven much, loves much" (Luke 7:47). Just as in each camp, our weakness is our strength misapplied. Though the Keepin' It Reals may cheapen grace, often, they champion God's grace because they truly do understand it in measures few of us do. They tend to be beautifully accepting and even gravitate toward the unlovely.

A Keepin' It Real's heart is genuinely poised for the good news of God's boundless love and lives it out with great acts of compassion. However, she'll pull away from Christians she finds hypocritical, judgmental, and unsafe. They're also often ripe for wide swings into the #Blessed campground, a far more attractive option! They're our final group of Christians.

—————————— ·•●•●•·· ——————————

The Keepin' It Reals

The Keepin' It Reals can be characterized by:

- Acting "free" (smiling and condescending to those still stuck in "being good").
- Being stuck in pet sins and feeling justified.
- Being grace-filled.
- Being more inclusive.

They can have thoughts like, or even express:

- "I don't need this. I can be a Christian without Christians."
- "It's all about grace. Truth's too hard to define."
- "Sorry, Lord" is their preface before doing something that's contrary to God's way.

Questions:

1. Does any of this sound familiar? Do you know the Keepin' It Reals?
2. What other characteristics would you add to the Keepin' It Reals?
3. Have you met a Keepin' It Real who you appreciate as a friend? What has been attractive about this person? Have there been any you want to avoid? If so, why?
4. If this sounds like you, write a few words or sentences expressing your feelings and/or thoughts on what you know of this category.

—————————— ·•●•●•·· ——————————

CHAPTER 7

#Blessed

"Did Jesus give you that? Well, I'll take Jesus." —John Piper[16]

While The Untapped, Truth Protectors, and Keepin' It Reals are busy reacting to each other, #Blessed smile and shake their heads, "Guys! This is good news!" And they're right—when we know God, there's so much to be happy about. We are chosen and called. There's no need to feel anxious about truth or fearful of heresy. We're no longer stuck in sin, and we can be authentic because we are fully known and fully loved. Our #Blessed friends smile and anticipate joy in Jesus. The only problem is sometimes their version of the Good News looks a bit like the American dream on steroids, in Jesus' name.

Who Are Our #Blessed?

There's a hope that's dangled before people who are struggling in life that has a sugarcoated "name it and claim it" impetus. Meaning, if you have enough faith, pray the right way, and name what you want, God will make it happen. God will "bless" you. It's often referred to as Prosperity Theology and the #Blessed crew subscribe heartily.

This group smiles a lot. They're very positive. So what's wrong with that? In this world of mass shootings and depression, a positive attitude is especially attractive.

People who struggle with relationships, finances, and, frankly, with life are often drawn to #Blessed, aka Prosperity Theology. Those who've climbed out of the rubble and are determined to have better find this camp very appealing. "God wants better for us. Think *bigger*: bigger careers, bigger ministries, bigger bank accounts."

Wealth

It's an oversimplification to say that Jesus wants us to live a richer lifestyle. Does he want us to have abundant life? Sure! But abundant spiritual life does not necessarily equate with comfort and ease and fancy clothes, cars and houses. In fact, Jesus had a lot to say about the perils of wealth.

I experienced this ideology firsthand while serving in a country in East Asia a couple of years ago.

Near the end of a three-day leadership training in one of the cities, I asked the women to outwardly express desires that God had given to them over our time together. One woman quickly responded: "I want a bigger house!"

I was quiet for a moment, considering. Then she said, "Oh, Nancy, that's the Prosperity Gospel, isn't it? I got tripped up. I know God wants bigger than that."

This beautiful woman course corrected in seconds. As a group, we didn't miss a beat and the spirit of the room was open and full of life. I simply said to her, "My love, you're beautiful and I love your heart. I agree, God wants so much more for us than that!"

Now, does God want to give her a bigger home? Maybe He does. But I find it curious that I hear far more stories of "God's" prompting for a bigger house (to use for ministry), than I do of His prompting to cap our lifestyle or downsize in order to use His resources (time, energy, emotional capacity, money) to serve and share as He directs.

God gives many good gifts that qualify as "good" by American standards. But the danger is in desiring God's good gifts above God Himself, the

Ultimate Gift. Often you can see signs of this idolatry (desiring anything above God) in the way we pray.

Prayer

Dr. Bruce Wilkinson's *The Prayer of Jabez* was released in 2000.[17] It topped the *New York Times* bestseller list and sold nine million copies in two years. People loved it. The little book was based on the portion of Scripture, 1 Chronicles 4:10: *"Jabez cried out to the God of Israel, 'Oh, that you would bless me and enlarge my territory! Let your hand be with me, and keep me from harm so that I will be free from pain.' And God granted his request."*

Christians from every walk of life were displaying the verse, memorizing and praying it. It was like a lucky charm.

I'm sure Dr. Wilkinson didn't anticipate such a reaction. He was probably just as shocked by the apparent Prosperity Theology rearing its ugly head. "God, go with me and protect me" *so that* I will be prosperous.

I find the same song, different verse among the prayers of many of my fellow Christians. Often we reduce prayer to "prayer requests." What is this? When will we get beyond this reduced idea of prayer, which reeks of, "give me"? One comedian quips, "I'm going upstairs to pray. Anybody want anything?" Ugh. The good news of God's presence calling us to praise Him for who He is, thank Him for what He's done and confess our sins to be refreshed again, has been reduced to God being my personal assistant.

"Oh, and God, make us all well. Wealthy? Heck yeah! And healthy."

#Blessed may misapply God's ways in the health department too.

Health

We live in a world where people still throw their garbage on the floors of movie theaters and in the stands at sporting events. I recently waded through as much garbage on the ground after a Philadelphia Penn's Landing Fireworks display as I have in the streets of some poor cities in the developing world.

We eat it too. Garbage, that is. And a lot of it.

Plus we're tired. I'm tired. We're constantly "on," overworked, and under-rested. We're under so much pressure from the sheer speed of life in the twenty-first century.

No wonder we're sick.

But #Blessed know that being sick isn't God's good plan.

From #Blessed, you may hear, "You won't get sick" or "the results will reverse" or "God *will* raise that woman up from her disease." And often God does. But not always. And that's the part that can get tricky with #Blessed. They often make assumptions as to why.

Christians who hover here aren't pulling their imbedded beliefs out of the sky. They, like the rest of us, love God, pray, and pour over the Scriptures.

Why #Blessed?

Scripture

As in the other camps, there's no shortage of Scripture that #Blessed draw on and live by.

In the Hebrew Scriptures (Old Testament):

- *"For I know the plans I have for you," declares the LORD, "plans to prosper you and not to harm you, plans to give you hope and a future"* (Jeremiah 29:11).

The Proverbs hold wisdom and promises around money and possessions:

- *"The blessing of the LORD brings wealth, without painful toil for it"* (Proverbs 10:22).
- *"Honor the LORD with your wealth, with the firstfruits of all your crops; then your barns will be filled to overflowing, and your vats will brim over with new wine"* (Proverbs 3:9-10).

Through the gospels and letters, these Christians hold to the promises of abundant life:

- *"With God, all things are possible!"* (Matthew 19:26).

- *"Now to Him who is able to do immeasurably more than all we ask or imagine, according to his power that is at work within us..."* (Ephesians 3:20).

So do we believe that or not?

And what about the various passages that flat out tell us, "ask whatever you wish for in my name and I will do it"? Jesus said that. And not just once.

They Were Rich

#Blessed defend a lavish, wealthy (or at least the dream of it) lifestyle by quoting passages like the above, and reminding us of biblical figures who prospered. Abraham, Job, and David are the gold standards. "See, God's ok with us being rich," they say.

But Jesus said, *"It is easier for a camel to go through the eye of a needle than for someone who is rich to enter the kingdom of God"* (Matthew 19:24). The truth is, women who are in North America are indeed rich compared to most of the world.

So I just wonder why the camel and the needle issue doesn't come up as much with these same rich American Christians.

There are five thousand references to the poor in Scripture (a matter clearly on God's heart and mind). Jesus instructed us to care for them (among others who are vulnerable). Should we gloss over His words to invest in the kingdom and travel light, *"'cause where your treasure is, there your heart will also be"* (Matthew 6:21)?

Reconciling Beliefs with Reality

Many people love and live beautifully for God and then suffer. What does #Blessed think of poor, but godly Christians? What about loving, attentive parents whose children die of depression that led to suicide? What do we do with godly, faithful sisters living in the poorest nations on earth?

#Blessed seem to position God as a means to treasure. What they're missing is that God is the treasure. Now, most Christians would declare that God and His glory are the goals. But in practice the emphasis is misplaced with #Blessed—their focus can be the benefits of belief and not relationship.

We Ask and God Gives Us Stuff

When things do not go well for you, how do you handle it? This is one of the ways you can tell whether, consciously or unconsciously, the #Blessed is where you tend to lean. Many who've adopted this theology walk away from God (literally or emotionally) when disaster comes. *God's not trustworthy after all,* they think.

My friend Karen came to know and follow Jesus after her husband left her for another woman. She and I grew to love each other through this time. She grew to draw on strength from God and other women she'd gathered in her home for a weekly Bible Study.

One evening sitting around her family room, I asked these highly educated career women "What is prayer?"

Karen answered, "It's asking God for stuff, and maybe He gives it to you. But maybe not." A very honest and telling statement.

This same woman called me crying one day, "Explain to me why my stupid husband and his new wife are happily doing just great, and why God's not"—despite her new and growing commitment to Him—'blessing' me. Why isn't God giving me a good job? Why can't I lose the weight? Why can't I find a great guy? Why am I having so many financial problems? Why, Nancy?! I thought loving and following Him would make life so much easier, but it's not true."

That's right. An easier, "better" life is not the goal. He is. He is the goal. That's the better Life. God will be with you in it all. He'll never leave you. While you walk through your years of highs and lows, I promise, with God you'll emerge as refined gold.

"Pure gold put in the fire comes out of it proved pure; genuine faith put through this suffering comes out proved genuine. When Jesus wraps this all up, it's

your faith, not your gold that God will have on display as evidence of his victory" (1Peter 1:7, The Message).

Often for #Blessed, these struggles are signs of lack of faith. *Don't let your faith waver. Don't let a shred of doubt or unbelief cloud how God wants to bless you.* This can set us up for a life of disappointment with God and with yourself.

Karen continued to follow Christ and love Him until she recently died at fifty-seven.

Where did Karen get her answer to the question I asked about prayer? In part, from some of the modeling done in Christian media.

Media

There's no shortage of #Blessed material gleaned from Christian media. Newspaper ads that sound like bad sales pitches indicating if you send in said amount, you'll get what you wish—uh—pray for.

Televangelists urging, "Send in your money. God wants to bless you, dear elderly woman on a fixed income. He'll bless you if you simply send us your money." God have mercy on us for this brand of gospel, which is no gospel at all (per Galatians 1:7).

Please hear me, I have no issue with Christian media. So much is good. And getting better. And of course media evangelists invite us to share in God's work with our resources. But it's a gross injustice to live a wealthy lifestyle of jets and mansions on the backs of poor, trusting, hopeful souls who are looking for genuine Life.

Desire Is Fine

Is there anything wrong with wanting your life to go well? Of course not. Everyone on the planet would prefer that.

God does want to bless us. But what do we do with Jesus, who suffered and called us to take up our crosses—our suffering and points of dying—and *still* follow Him?

As with each group I've identified, our #Blessed certainly bring to the Church much good.

Strengths

Freedom

I lived the first half of my life in Toronto, Canada. The "Toronto Blessing," a place of extraordinary revival (now Airport Christian Fellowship church) was in full force. I visited a few times, knowing that Christians traveled there from across the world because of the outpouring of God's Spirit on that place.

The first night I visited the gathering, I was intrigued and utterly delighted.

There was a freedom of worship: children running around with long, flowing ribbons, dancing, people sitting, standing, clapping, arms down or way, way up—it didn't matter!

This was new for me. Pregnant with our first son, I sat in the back of the large warehouse space, on the floor, with my head in my knees. I prayed, "Lord, I know nothing of this. This isn't my experience of you and church. But if this is you, I want in."

I've been to several other #Blessed gatherings over the years. Freedom is often a hallmark of their gatherings.

Faith

The faith I've seen from these Christians is often better than anywhere else I've seen in the Church. #Blessed take Jesus' mission, "Thy kingdom come on earth as it is in heaven," to heart. They go for it!

I've heard countless stories of God's increase of faith on men and women who've been delivered from illnesses, healed from blindness, raised from the dead, cured from diseases, freed from addictions, you name it. You may balk, but I've heard testimonies of doctors shaking their heads with, *no hope, no way, no how*, until a group of #Blessed believed and God did something extraordinary.

Everywhere I go in the world, I pray, "Please God, show me your glory in this way." But the #Blessed don't just pray and hear about it and imagine what it could be like—they live it!

As you'd expect, there's a heaping amount of joy in our #Blessed.

Joy

These congregations I've ministered in—charismatic, Pentecostal, the "healing" stream of Christianity—have been some of the most joyful, fun, and loving I've encountered anywhere. It's a delight for me to be included in any and every denomination, but these guys are a trip! There's an exuberance and generosity of spirit that's so uplifting. And as with each camp I've described, they add immeasurably to the Church.

···•●●●•···

#Blessed

#Blessed can be characterized by:

- Being expressive and joyful.
- Naming and claiming prosperity—health, wealth, children, success.
- Challenging any hint of suffering or negative ideas.
- Using spiritual bypass (avoiding genuine disappointment with lofty spiritual talk and ideas).
- An awareness and experience of healing gifts.
- Being assertive in their belief that God will act.

They may have thoughts like, or even express:

- "We have the full gospel."
- When struggles come, they look for excuses: "Do you have traces of this in your family?" "What did you do?" Or "What haven't you done?" Assumptions are made to explain, "why?"
- "Don't you speak that!" Meaning, they don't like to hear anything that's not positive.

Questions:

1.   Does any of this sound familiar? Do you know the #Blessed?

2.   What other characteristics would you add to the #Blessed?

3.   Reflect on where any of the #Blessed characteristics have had a positive/negative impact on your relationships.

4.   If this sounds like you, write a few words or sentences expressing your feelings and/or thoughts on what you know of this kind of Christian.

———————————————— ••●●●●•• ————————————————

CHAPTER 8

Rag Rights

"Why would a princess put on an old dress
To dance with her beloved and the chance to catch His eye?"
—*Nichole Nordeman*[18]

I've identified four different "camps" that have assembled in the Church today:

- The Untapped
- The Truth Protectors
- The Keepin' it Reals
- The #Blessed

Over and over as I write, I'm confronted with the fact that there is no easy diagnosis. No simple solutions. I'm aware that what I write is a snapshot and is not, by any means, the whole picture.

Hopefully, you're not full on, habitually camping out. Sure, maybe you have a tendency to lean in one direction, but my prayer is that you're much more engaged in the Good News of life than you are in camping out in the ditch.

But what if you are? Camping out, that is. What if you did recognize yourself in one of these four descriptions?

You may be thinking, "Darn right I am! You have no idea what I've endured. It's a new day, and I'm livin' large!"

Or, "I do see my leaning. And I like it. I do protect truth and we need that today!"

Or, "Shoot, I *am* wallowing in my lowliness and sin."

Or, finally, "What if I try a different approach and I just can't do it?"

Each of the four camps illustrates ways we've learned to cope. Ways we've defended. Ways we've protected our own fear and shame. If you're able to see it—however you feel about it—that's a gift. It's a start.

The truth is, we all have a bit of each of these camps going on. Many have also done wide swings from one camp to another. I've met previously Untapped people whose pendulum has swung to #Blessed. And Truth Protectors who, after a crisis or serious moral failure become Keepin' it Reals.

I want to address something you may have noticed in all four camps. I'm addressing it because it can be a dividing matter in the Church.

About Scripture

Did you notice that Scripture was the basis for each camp? Does that bother you? Don't let it. It's an age-old issue that scholars and theologians and the most phenomenal followers of Christ have not settled. (And won't until Christ's return.) It's why humility and generosity across the Church are so critical.

On a practical note, it's also a good reminder to look at each passage of Scripture in the context of the whole Bible. We take into consideration the literary (genre, authorship), historical, and theological contexts.

Not everything in Scripture is *prescribing*, but often simply *describing* what happened. So many Christians get tripped up on that. Not everything that happened in Scripture is normative. ("It happened that way for them, it'll happen that way for us.") God is far too creative and surprising for that! And remember: The Scriptures were intended to be read primarily in community. Think that through. It has many implications.

This or That?

Dividing into our "camps" is not a new issue for anyone, including Christians. There's nothing new under the sun. But I believe with all my heart, God is calling us to see this in fresh light.

So we can keep hanging out in our camps. Keep stoking the fires of our fallenness and brokenness. Keep rehashing the same old stories that anger and annoy.

Or.

Or we can give up our "rag rights" (Oswald Chambers, *My Utmost for His Highest*) and move toward God as He calls us to Life. [19]

I don't know about you, but I choose life.

CHAPTER 9

Where Are You?

"What you are looking for is where you are looking from."
—St. Francis of Assisi

D o you agree with what I'm saying regarding the Church's division of "camps"? What about the general preoccupation with the bad news? I want to remind you of God's overarching, or core calling that goes out to all creation: *"Then the man and his wife heard the sound of the LORD God as He was walking in the garden in the cool of the day, and they hid from the LORD God among the trees of the garden. But the LORD God called to the man, 'Where are you?'"* (Genesis 3: 8-9).

Where *Are* You?

You ask that question when you can't find someone. Where are you? But the issue here isn't lack of knowledge. God knew their location.

You ask, "Where are you?" when what was, is no more. Lying in bed beside your spouse of nine years, who's preoccupied with his career. He comes home distracted. Present in the body, but not really there. You share a story, but he's checking his phone. He doesn't seem present to your needs. *Where are you*, you wonder.

You ask that question when you're angry or annoyed. Where *are* you?

But anger is rooted in fear, and annoyance is attached to demands. "You're not here. You should be here!" is the underlying message.

But God's call is none of these.

Lost Child

I once lost our son David while we were at the mall. I pushed my boys in a double stroller. One-year-old Aaron was lying in the back, but David wanted to get out. He was three.

"Ok, buddy, but stay close to mom," I cautioned.

Inside a department store, I rummaged through a sales rack. David impishly ducked in and out from around the stroller and under the round clothing racks.

I kept watch on both boys, while trying to find a good deal.

A moment later, "David?"

No response.

"David?"

Still nothing.

My eyes darted around the store. I pulled back clothes on the racks to see if my playful boy was hiding. My heart pounded as mother instincts kicked into high gear.

"Please help me find my little boy," I pleaded with anyone in sight.

Any parent who's ever had that experience understands, "Where are you?" is the caring, loving, "come back!" call of a parent who loves beyond words.

That's what it's like, though God's not frantic. He knows all and is in complete control. His boundless, protective love is like that. God's been that loving, protective Parent ever since that Genesis 3 scene.

Calling His Church

God is calling His Church to come back. Come back to Life. The Church around the globe that I've had the honor of serving is growing and building. But the Church in my own backyard is not.

You know as well as I do that the Church is made up of people. You and I. We are the Church. Whether we meet in a coffee shop, a field, a home or a "traditional" building. We are the Church. Church transformation begins with personal transformation. A collective call to Life! Those who study organization and cultural change know that organizations don't transform. People do.

Unless we're apathetic or oblivious, we cringe. *What's happening? Where's the Church?*

My dear sister, you are the Church. The question is: Where are you?

You Are Here

If it's true that we grope around in the lowlands instead of embracing life, our starting place is to identify where we are. With that clarity, we can move forward with confidence.

Think about heading out for a hike in a State Park. When you get to the park, say you want to find a particular gorge, waterfall, or lookout. What do you do? You go to the directory and locate the desired area. Great, so you know where you're going, but what's next? You need to find the red dot. The little red dot that indicates: You Are Here.

So where are you?

God

Where are you with God? Think about it. Today (these days), where are you with God? Not "where were you" when you were a kid. Not "where were you" as a passionate teen. Where *are* you?

Now, you may be thinking, *I'm good with God. I'm a Christian. My grandparents never miss a day of mass or church. We're Christian. But, I mean, I'm not like, really serious or a fanatic or anything.*

Maybe you're wondering, *what God are we talking about?*

Or perhaps you're fine with God, but the Church has you a bit turned off.

Maybe you're on fire! Your heart's aligned with God's heart. You're big-time alive!

Regardless of where you are on the spectrum, own it.

Camps

Do you see yourself in any of the camps? Are you aware of where you tend to lean and do you know why that may be the case?

Hopefully the work you've done on each of the chapters to identify where you may fall was helpful for you. You may have all kinds of feelings around what you discovered.

You're not alone. We don't live in isolation. We live in community, invited into God's family, called the Church.

The Church

Many would give a collective nod to the apparent decline of the church in North America. We can see the dwindling congregations. But here's what the experts say.

Decline

- U.S. adults who say they regularly attend religious services continues to decline (*Why Americans Go [and Don't Go] to Religious Services*).[20]
- Americans are attending church less, and more people are experiencing and practicing their faith outside of its four walls. Millennials in particular are coming of age at a time of great skepticism and cynicism toward institutions—particularly the church (David Kinnaman with Barna).[21]

Six in ten young people will leave the church permanently or for an extended period starting at age fifteen . . . and it's more than the usual 'driver's license to marriage license' joy ride . . ."[22]

Whether they're called *unchurched, dechurched, nones,* or *unaffiliated,* people are less inclined to be included in the American church.

You may say, "Sure, the numbers are down, but God's not all about numbers."

You're absolutely right. He's calling us to Life through obedience and holiness.

Pound for Pound? Same.

From a statistical perspective, it's difficult to distinguish Christians and non-Christians. Other than Christians owning more Bibles, going to Church, and attending more church events, we function the same as non-Christians. The rates of divorce, addictions, abuse, etc. are virtually the same (George Barna, Pastor's Conference).[23]

Christians I speak to all over North America respond to this predicament with some combination of:

- Resignation. "Well, sure, America's going to hell in a handbasket."
- Disgust. "What's the matter with these people?"
- Blame. "I blame it on . . ." And the list is varied: Blame it on democrats, Donald Trump, Me Too, or white men. Blame it on Catholics, Episcopalians or fundamentalists. But the message is, "Someone better answer for this!"

And into all of this, just as He did in the Garden, God calls: "Where are you?"

Questions

1. In what ways do you agree with what I'm saying regarding the Church's division of "camps"? What about the general preoccupation with the "bad news"? Do you agree or disagree?

2. Where are you in terms of the Church? How do you feel? What experiences have shaped your thoughts, ideas, feelings?

3. Spend some time praying about the Church here and around the world.

Part 2

LIVING IN LIGHT OF THE GOOD NEWS

"The waters are rising, but so am I. I am not going under, but over."
—Catherine Booth

CHAPTER 10

Core Calling

"And as You speak, a hundred billion creatures catch Your breath."
—*"So Will I," Hillsong Joel Houston / Benjamin Hastings / Michael Fatkin*[24]

Long before God called us back to Himself, he called us forth from nothing.

God called everything into existence. He called forth the light, the day, the planets, sea and sky. Every living thing originated by His call.

He simply said, "Let there be," and there was. (Genesis 1)

Remarkable

Vegetation alone is remarkable. Dr. David Bradstreet writes: "Our planet is home to some 10 to 14 million species of living things . . . Few of us ever stop to think about the power of plants, but a recent column in the *New York Times* hailed them for being 'as close to biological miracles as a scientist could dare admit.' As Douglas Tallamy writes, 'After all, they allow us to eat sunlight . . . and plants also produce oxygen, build topsoil and hold it in place, prevent floods, sequester carbon dioxide, buffer extreme weather and clean our water.' Life thrives even in the deepest and darkest regions of the ocean floor, where no sunshine ever permeates the gloom. Strange plants grow 20,000 feet below the surface, surviving on chemical nutrients emerging from vents in the ocean floor."[25]

That blows my mind! I'm nowhere close to a science buff, but that level of specificity around plant life astounds me.

God imagined, created, then breathed life into every living creature. He called us to life then, and He calls us to life now. It's what I call the core calling that goes out to all.

Know God

I'll reiterate how author and social critic, Os Guinness defines this core calling (or what he calls, Primary calling) which I cited in my Introduction: *To know God and make Him known.* That's it. Know God. The focus is not on "head knowledge," though that's part of it, of course. Think experience. *Experience God.*

But how do you know/experience God? We experience God by interacting with Scripture. We experience God through praying in new or ancient ways. We experience God by enjoying diversity in people. Pay attention to what's right in front of you. Experience the smell of lavender and lemon, the taste of salt and ginger. Go walking among redwood forests. Oh my goodness, have you ever been to Cathedral forest in western Canada? It's on Vancouver Island. Stunning! You arch your neck, nearly falling back, straining to catch a glimpse of the tops of those trees that seem to go for miles! Right up to the sky. God draws us up, up, higher and higher . . .

Experience God in these and a million other ways, and when you do, life will pour out of you!

Their Sound Has Gone Out

God magnifies His call through what He creates and sustains: *"The heavens declare the glory of God; the skies proclaim the work of his hands. Day after day they pour forth speech; night after night they reveal knowledge. They have no speech, they use no words; no sound is heard from them. Yet their voice goes out into all the earth, their words to the ends of the world"* (Psalm 19:1-4).

Centuries later, the apostle Paul, a stellar Jewish Pharisee turned Christ-follower, echoes this Psalm in his letter to the Romans: *"But I ask: Did they not hear?* [God's call] *Of course they did: 'Their voice has gone out into all the earth, their words to the ends of the world'"* (Romans 10:18).

A core calling to all! It's not the specific, tailor-made calling (a secondary or personal calling), but the primary call to simply *receive* from God.

These are invitations to come alive.

Sometimes it starts in the head and moves to the heart. If you're analytical, mathematical, scientific, chances are you'll "hear" God's call first in your head. Sometimes the opposite is true. If you're like me, it often begins in your heart and makes its way up to your noggin. Either way, who cares? The point is you're experiencing the call of God.

Come to me and live!

More foundational still is this: beyond our feelings and deep thoughts, our involuntary chills down the spine, or unexpected tear that trickled at these signs of life, is our longing. We know there's more. We know God's drawing us higher and it compels us to respond.

A Response

This core calling blankets all creation. It's as pervasive as the air you and I breathe. Some brush this notion off as sentimental. Others perceive it and positively respond. Look how the apostles Paul and Peter wrote about those of us who positively responded: *"All things work together for good for **those who love God**, who are called according to his purpose"* (Romans 8:28, emphasis mine).

"Live lives worthy of God who calls you into his kingdom and glory" (1 Thessalonians 2:12).

"His divine power has given us everything we need for a godly life through our knowledge of him who called us by his own glory and goodness" (2 Peter 1:3).

This calling originates from a God of love, purpose, and life and goes out to all creation.

But when it comes to humanity, this call's in a league of its own.

CHAPTER 11

How Then Shall We Live?

"He called you to this through our Gospel, that you might share in the glory of our Lord Jesus Christ." —2 Thessalonians 2:14

I've been in the church a long time. I started following Jesus around when I was just a toddler. Yes, you read that right: a toddler. And I had nothing to do with it.

My father was a Christian. When it came to his treatment of women, he didn't exactly emulate the character of Christ but he self-identified as "Christian" just the same.

Still, he was the one who said to my very non-Christian mom, "I want to take the kids to church."

To which my mother replied, "Fine. But don't bring that garbage home to me."

My mother was a party girl. Not sex, drugs, and alcohol kinda' party girl. She just enjoyed a good time! She was a go-getter and full of excitement and vigor. She wasn't going to let anyone get in the way of that. Especially God. *God could really get in the way of a good time. Cramp my style, rain on my parade,* she thought.

So off we went to church at The Salvation Army in Owen Sound, Canada: Dad, Karen, Debra, and the baby, eighteen-month-old me. Mom stayed home.

Alive!

Up to that point, I was fairly nonverbal. Now, I don't know how verbal you're supposed to be by eighteen months, but developmentally speaking, whatever my two older sisters were, I apparently was not. The extent of my vocabulary was, "No." Mom thought there must be something wrong with me. "Poor little thing, she's not pretty *and* she's slow." But the story goes from mom's perspective: "Nancy, the day you came home from church for the first time, you came home singing about Jesus. Not just speaking, but singing! And you never stopped. Child, you lit up like a Christmas tree!"

Mom loved to recount how the life in me never dwindled. In fact, I was so alive, so changed, so different, she was intrigued. So she followed me to church, and there learned that God wasn't mad at her at all, and that in fact, He loved her.

God loved her.

He wasn't trying to squelch her vigor and life, but wanted her to have that life full-on. It was a totally different message than what she'd believed for so long. At thirty-eight, she ended up following Jesus for the rest of her eighty years.

Since that first time hearing of Jesus, I've loved and followed Him. And at eighteen months, what did I know? I didn't "decide" or fall on my knees and cry out to God. He just came to me. Called me to life. *Little lamb, you're mine.*

Now, through my over forty years of following Jesus, have I had to deal with deep-seated issues? Oh yeah. Daddy issues, for sure. And much of what I've shared in this book is how God patiently and profoundly heals me. But through thick and thin, my passion for God, and for others to see Him has only increased.

I can't explain it. I can't comprehend it. But like the story of sleeping beauty, God came and kissed me. And brought me to life. It's a mystery to me how God does this.

Here's another mystery.

The Mystery

Again we look back at the apostle Paul's letter to the early Christians: *"[I] present to you the word of God in its fullness—the mystery that has been kept hidden for ages and generations, but is now disclosed to the Lord's people. To them God has chosen to make known among the Gentiles the glorious riches of this mystery, which is* **Christ in you, the hope of glory**" (Colossians 1:25-27, emphasis mine).

Did you catch the mystery that had been kept secret? The secret hidden for "ages and generations"? Here it is: *Christ in you, the hope of glory.*

Now, just a few verses later he writes, "*the mystery of God, namely, Christ*" (Colossians 2:2), so we know this incredible mystery has everything to do with Jesus, the Christ. (Christ is a title, not Jesus' last name).

But in that first Colossians passage (1:25-27), he writes that the mystery is the word of God *in its fullness.* That is Jesus, who is the Living Word of God (John 1:1, 14), and the spirit of that living Word of God, *in you.*

In Its Fullness

Pause and take that in. *Christ in you, the hope of glory.*

If you're like me, you need to read it over. Insert the personal pronoun: *Christ in ME, the hope of glory.*

The Word of God "in its fullness" gets expressed in the millions of God's people. We carry in us the Spirit of Christ. We make up The Body of Christ. Also known as His Church. When we're really living it, there is nothing more extraordinary, more beautiful, more glorious, than our full-on selves—the Body of Christ—demonstrating the glorious power of God!

This glorious power is the Gospel.

Tell Me Something I Don't Know

If you're getting that tell-me-something-I-don't-know attitude as you read this, what a tragedy. But you're not alone. I have to admit, there've been times I've sat in church services where the pastor's message is the basic Gospel, and I've thought, *oh, come on, we know this. Give us something meaty. Something new.*

I've then quickly caught myself: *What? Something meatier than the Gospel? Something a little more exciting, Nancy? Good grief.*

If you were raised on this message, it's easy to overlook foundational truths. And applying the truth? Please! Now that changes everything.

I don't care if you're a seasoned Christian or someone who knows zilch about Jesus. Every one of us needs the reality of the Gospel driven deeper and deeper. Daily.

The Gospel

So in light of this Colossians text, let's look again at the Gospel in a classic structure:

1. Creation—God created all things and they were good. Very good. God, the Trinity, then crowned all creation with God's masterpiece: humanity. He crowned them with glory (Genesis 1:27; Psalm 8:4-8; Acts 17:28). God, and those first humans enjoyed intimacy right from the start. In this perfect relationship, humanity was fully alive. And glorious.

2. The Fall (Divorce)—There was a rupture in the relationship between God and all creation. Why? Because we went our own way (Genesis 3). Autonomy, or self-rule, is the essential issue that caused a break in this original relationship between God and people (Isaiah 53:6). God says, "This is what's good and true." We say, "I'll decide what's good and true . . . for me." That dynamic has been separating humanity from the God who is Life ever since. The glory of people is still present, (everyone's still made in the image of God) but it's marred. Veiled. A shadow of its former self. Do you know anyone who thinks life is perfect? Everywhere you look, all you've experienced in this world has been disfigured by this broken relationship. Flowers fade. Sharks attack. People betray. Babies die. Going our own way meant separation from the God who is Life. The cost? Death.

3.   Jesus—But God's solution to the problem is Jesus. Jesus—God in a skin suit, God incognito—got up from His throne, took off His royal robe, and came to earth. He lived the perfect life we could never live, and died the death we should have died. But why? Love. Perfect Love, the only perfect sacrifice to pay the very high cost of sin (Romans 6:23). Only Jesus could then enter into death (on a cross) in order to overcome it from within, so that in *everything*—even death—He would reign and rule (Colossians 1:15). We're made eternally alive by the Life of God (His Spirit) in us. We're made glorious once more! And we constantly increase in glory (2 Corinthians 5:17; Galatians 2:20).

4.   Restoration—There will come a day when God will completely restore all the earth. All worry and grief, fatigue and pressure will be gone. There will be no more tears. Lions and lambs will get along. So will democrats and republicans. All that we see now will be completely and totally restored. Humanity and all creation will be glorious! (2 Corinthians 3:7-18, Colossians 3:3, 4).

From that Genesis 3 scene, throughout all Scripture, the message is this: God relentlessly goes to every length to bring us back to Life.

Regardless of where you stand on that, you should know that I've just explained the overarching theme of the whole Bible. The main message people across every continent of the world have lived for. And died for. For over two thousand years.

Let's Break It Down

In short, the Gospel looks like this: Good news, bad news, good news, good news.

- Creation—Good News
- Fall—Bad News
- Jesus—Good News
- Restoration—Good News

Again—good news, bad news, good news, good news.

The Gospel really is the ultimate *good* news.

But wait. There's more. What else did you notice? Do you see a truth in the Gospel you may have missed before?

Think back to the Colossians passage, "*Christ in you, the hope of glory*". Notice the glory of God's people, in and through the Gospel:

1. Creation—Good News—Humanity is created glorious.
2. Fall—Bad News—Humanity's glory is marred. All people still bear the image of God, (the Imago Dei), but our glory is veiled.
3. Jesus—Good News—In and through Jesus Christ, we are made gloriously alive once more. And that glory only increases until . . .
4. Restoration—Good News—When all is said and done, and God establishes His full reign "on earth as it is in heaven," humanity will be fully glorified. Fully perfected. Fully alive.

That's 75%!

Even I can do the math on this one. That's 75% of the overarching theme of the Bible that is actual good news. And a major part of that good news involves your glory. You are glorious. Together we display God's glory as "the word of God *in its fullness* . . ."

Who doesn't want this? Who doesn't want to know they're striking, magnificent, glorious? Who doesn't want to live like that?

Truth be told, from where many stand it seems a lot of us. Too much of the Church is sloshing around in the 25% bad news, instead of living in light of this Good News.

Let's go after this!

CHAPTER 12

The Power of the Cross

"Death is crushed to death, life is mine to live."
—"The Power of the Cross" by the Gettys[26]

God powerfully saves us one time for all. Then saves us over and over. The cross is God's gift that keeps on giving.

"God rescued us from dead-end alleys and dark dungeons. He's set us up in the kingdom of the Son he loves so much, the Son who got us out of the pit we were in, and got rid of the sins we were doomed to keep repeating" (Colossians 1:13-14, The Message).

As we look at our propensity to camp out, huddling in our echo chambers, frustrating and confusing everybody, one thing's for sure: it probably traces back to a misunderstanding of the Gospel.

The Fault Line

When I was singing professionally, if I had trouble with a song or put stress on my voice, my voice teacher would inevitably take me back to basics: Breathing, mouth positions, oohing and aahing. These would expose bad habits and ways I compensated. This is true regardless of the discipline—math, sports, business, communication—and at any level of proficiency. If you're struggling, chances are that going back to basics will reveal where there's a disconnect. The same is true for Christians and the Gospel.

Cross Chart

Years ago, pastor and author Jack Miller wrote a course called, "Sonship" in which he addressed basic issues that were spiritually butchering many of the missionaries he visited around the world.[27] He encountered team dissention, marital strain, bummed out, burned out men and women of God. These were themes and variations he'd seen from those who'd given their lives—left homes and families—to share God's love. He developed this course to drive them back to God's power that saves and keeps us.

The Cross Chart

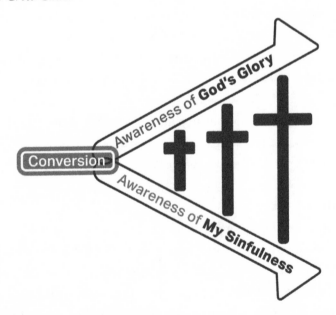

Point of Conversion

This diagram describes the journey from the point a person says "yes" to God's gift of forgiveness of our sin, and to becoming leader of our lives.

(Conversion). Some have a clear date and time when that happened for them. Others can't tell you when and where, but they know they're a child of God based on what Christ has done. They love and follow Him.

From that point on, the unending Life of God, the Holy Spirit comes inside. Deeper, stronger transforming work begins. Awareness of two things is critical for this transforming work.

Awareness of God's Glory (Holiness)

Take a look at the rising line on the chart. As we grow, we have an increased awareness of God: His holiness, beauty, grace, power, mercy, and so on. It's an increased awareness of His glory. The more we enjoy God and know Him through prayer, Scripture, the Church, and living it out with people far from Him, the more we become aware of His glory.

At the same time we grow in an awareness of our sin.

Awareness of My Sin

Notice the downward line. This shows the ever-increasing awareness of our sin. (Oh, goodie.) This sounds bleak, but believe it or not, the awareness of sin increases as we grow in Christ and become more mature in our faith. (Stay with me.)

Now, if we only looked at our sin, we're goners. We may as well pack it in and go home. This part of the Gospel is the bad news. The depth of our sin extends beyond what we can imagine. (The things we've done, left undone, attitudes no one else knows about—all of it is *going our own way*.) So we see it. And we shudder.

Look how wide the difference is between God's glory and our sin. It's the awareness of these two things that makes us conscious of the gap.

But then . . .

Crossing The Great Divide

Look at the cross. As we live aware of distance between God's perfection and our own, we get desperate until we realize that's precisely why Christ came—to bridge that gap! The awareness of the divide habitually connects us to our need.

Remember the lyric from "Amazing Grace": "'Twas grace that taught my heart to fear (the gift of our awareness of sin), and grace my fears relieved"? (God's gift of the cross!) The Cross Chart is a fantastic representation of that phrase. It's the power of the cross.

As we're honest about our sin, and about who God is in His unrivalled glory, the cross increases more and more. It's not actually enlarging. It's already full size. Its work is full and complete. But as we continue to access it in our lives, we realize more of its power.

When you get this, it's what makes you throw up your hands in worship: "Hallelujah!" That's the power of the cross!

My former pastor, the late Rich Craven, would often say, "For every one look you take at yourself, take nine at the cross." That ratio keeps God and His saving power always front and center.

What's Your Focus?

The Untapped may be focusing too much on sin. That'll keep a person down for sure. It's time to look up!

Truth Protectors have a tendency to avoid the genuine ugliness of our sin. *I'm a good girl, I have sound theology,* leads to lessening the range between God's glory and our sin. So in theory, the cross is good, but in reality, doesn't really seem necessary.

Keepin' It Reals neglect God's glory through transformation, missing the cross's power to renovate our lives.

#Blessed may have a hyper focus on God's glory, but don't take an honest assessment of their own sin, preferring to always focus on the positive, using hyper spiritual language.

In any of these groups, there's an imbalance on focus. Get honest about your sin, but look up! As you do, be amazed by God and His provision in the cross.

I love how seventeenth century author and philosopher Soren Kierke-gaard kept the focus: "Father in Heaven! Hold not our sins up against us but hold us up against our sins so that the thought of You when it wakens in our soul, and each time it wakens, should not remind us of what we have committed but of what You did forgive, not of how we went astray but of how You did save us!"[28]

What does this actually look like?

An Ordinary Day

One day, I stood rifling through the cheese section in Trader Joe's, just minding my own business, making my selection of Extra Sharp Cheddar and Blue. Then, snap! An adulterous thought came to me. Zipped right into my mind. Prompted by absolutely nothing. I wasn't standing in the checkout with seedy images taunting me, or finding an old boyfriend on Facebook.

This and countless temptations come into our minds every day.

Here are some typical responses:

- The Untapped: "I'm such a sinner."
- Truth Protectors: "Of course, I'm a sinner." Then secretly beat themselves up, "When will I ever be holy?"
- Keepin' It Reals: "I can't help it. I am who I am. Maybe I'll even go there. God's grace will cover me."
- #Blessed: "I triumph over that kind of thinking. I'm more than a conqueror!"

None of these actually deals with the issue by releasing the resurrection power that is in us.

What Do We Do?

So what do we do? We look sin square in the face and pray something like this: "God, I see it too. I confess this (adulterous) thought. I agree with you. It's not the real me in you. God, please put your healing touch on that place in me that's broken and susceptible. Increase the resurrection power that's in me, in that very place. Amen."

Then move on!

Until you face the depth of your sin, and the cross of Christ that increases to absorb and transform it, you will never, *never* live into who God's called and created you to be.

God's glory becomes your glory through the cross.

Here's the process at a glance:

- Get honest: Acknowledge and confess the issue (your sin).
- Look at God. (God's glory).
- Receive the great exchange in the cross: Your sin for His holiness and glory.
- Thank God and move on!

Don't get sucked into playing games about your sin. It just distracts you from what's yours through the cross.

A Note About Forgiveness

In this chapter I'm focusing on personal sin and the forgiveness you receive from God. There are times when deeper, more intensive work is needed. (We'll get to that in the next couple of chapters.) But this is the basic implementation of the Gospel. Don't fall into making this more complicated than it needs to be. That prolongs the pain, and I believe it's one of the reasons many Christians muck about in the bad news. If we avoid dealing with our sin, we may also be (unconsciously) incessantly paying penance.

A swift dealing with our own sin—with God and the one offended (which involves more nuances), brings us back to the power of the cross that sets us free.

Yes, it takes humility and courage. (Good. We need these as followers of Christ.) This is basic application. Because all of life is repentance, my sister: a turning away in order to turn toward.

All Of Life Is Repentance

The truth is we're all guilty. You can take that in and let it crush you, or you can face it and let the Good News of Jesus Christ crush the hell right out of it!

Let's take a page from the Early Church.

The Early Church

The early monastics were groups of people in seclusion. (Monks, nuns, etc.) They were communities devoted to holy living. You might be interested to know that they would be perplexed by what they see in many Christians today when it comes to sin. They knew they'd mess up. It was written, *"for all have sinned and fall short of the glory of God"* (Romans 3:23). They weren't so shocked, so in despair, nor so cavalier. Issues of sin were handled swiftly.

Retired Professor and author Roberta Bondi writes that "confession of guilt was something quite different to our monastic ancestors. It was a freeing experience that cut them loose from the weight of the past in order to be able to begin each day as the start of a new unburdened life."

Getting honest about our failings requires humility. "Humility," writes Bondi, "has no self-image to maintain. It does not, out of embarrassment, hide its sin, and it is ever watchful to escape it. But when sin occurred for the ancient monastic there was, theoretically at least, no temptation to deny it, no temptation to beat the breast and say, 'How could I have done such a thing?' The answer was well known already. 'I did it because I, too, am a creature, subject to sin.' Pervasive guilt, self-loathing, despair over a committed sin, these were not problems to those able to confess, repent and receive forgiveness."[29]

The Apostle Paul

Paul expressed this same concept to Timothy, *"Here is a trustworthy saying that deserves full acceptance: Christ Jesus came into the world to save sinners—of whom I am the worst"* (1Timothy 1:15). As with all Scripture, you can't isolate one verse from the rest of the Bible. Notice this verse against the fullness of Paul's life as described throughout the New Testament:

- His life was radically changed when he encountered Jesus.
- He devoted his life to proclaiming the Gospel.
- He took huge missionary journeys.
- He started many churches.
- He wrote most of the New Testament.
- He suffered beatings, poisonous snake bites, shipwrecks, imprisonment, and kept on preaching, *"For me to live is Christ!"*

Unlike many Christians today who allow this "worst of sinners" to grab them by the throat, Paul was not struggling to be alive in his life. He didn't let his recognition of his sin pull him down. He wasn't paralyzed by his sin. It served as the backdrop of immeasurable grace and his desperate need of a Savior. *"Who will rescue me from this body of sin?"* Paul wrote. *"Thanks be to God through Jesus Christ our Lord!"* (Romans 7:24).

Then he packed up and headed out to live the Good News!

The answer to being gloriously alive in the power of the cross is not to ignore or minimize issues. It's to face them. Let's take this further.

CHAPTER 13

Get Honest

"To know the truth is to see accurately. To believe what isn't true is to be blind."
—*Randy Alcorn*[30]

The Church has done astounding good over the last two thousand years. It's true. Because of the love of God and our desire to express this love in word and deed (the Gospel), people's lives have been changed for good. Alive in Christ, we've moved out.

Good Work

We've served the hungry and broken. Moved toward the marginalized of society in prisons, shelters, hospitals, and orphanages. We bind the wounds of the suffering at times of war and natural catastrophes.

I love an ad I saw put out by The Salvation Army (known for rolling up their sleeves and moving toward tough stuff for Christ). The ad is an image of a young woman walking through wreckage of torn trees and collapsed houses, an area clearly destroyed by a hurricane. The caption? "We combat natural disasters with acts of God." True!

The stories of villages, cities, and whole nations being saved by God's people moving into action are countless and span the centuries.

A Remote Village

Remember the east Asian country I mentioned earlier, where the pastor faced a man at gunpoint to bring the Gospel to a remote village? He was told, "Stop preaching this message or die." Well, he didn't stop preaching. And he didn't die. Four years later, that pastor took me to that village to meet the first family that received God's love through Christ. Then I got to meet all the villagers who now also love and follow Him!

For the glory of God, Christ-followers started educational institutions like our illustrious Ivey League schools—Harvard University, Yale and Princeton, Dartmouth as examples.

How many hospitals and global clinics are given names that identify them as Christian?

The truth is that by God's grace and power, we have lived out the mission God gave us. We have lived out Christ's command to, *"let your light shine before others, that they may see your good deeds and glorify your Father in heaven"* (Matthew 5:16).

This is true. And I've only begun to touch on the good that's been done. But there are other truths to face.

Not Good

I have no desire to discourage. And bashing the Church is never my goal. But getting honest about where we're failing is desperately needed.

Why would followers of Jesus Christ—created, called, and empowered by His Life in us—*choose* to live in light of the bad news instead of the good?

There are lots of reasons.

In the earlier chapter titled, "Where Are You?" I suggested that taking a look at ourselves and where we tend to "camp out" is critical if we're going to live into our glorious calling. That chapter deals with the "where." Where are you? Where do you see yourself?

Now I'd like to look at the "why?" Why are you where you are? We want to get honest about why we think and feel the way we do. Why we've camped out or walked out. But we don't want to deal with this at arm's length. We need to get up close and personal. I'll warn you: this is not a feel-good section. But it is honest.

Avalanche

The foreign film *Force Majeure* tells of a rather underwhelming avalanche that shakes up a French family while on a little ski getaway in the Alps.

Movie reviewer Ella Taylor writes, "A successful businessman who seems equally pleased with his good looks and his cell phone, Tomas, has come to this pricy resort to relax with his trophy wife, Ebba, and their two children. They make a sleek, perfect domestic unit in a perfect, smooth-running hotel, all clean lines and blond wood."[31]

The family was taking a break from the slopes and enjoying lunch out on the sunny terrace when they casually noticed the rising mist and buckling snow atop a nearby mountain. Huh . . . some activity. Everyone noticed and heard the seemingly distant, insignificant avalanche, but no one really reacted. They were virtually certain the avalanche wouldn't affect they're lovely lunch. Wrong. The avalanche did in fact make its way right down and across the terrace. Everyone clamored, reaching for their children and running for cover.

Within minutes the avalanche was over, and the slightly disheveled diners returned to the terrace. Lunch was snowed under. Bummer. But here's the issue: Ebba jumped up and began to reach for her children. Before she could even grab their second child then run for cover, Tomas had simply hightailed it out of there. Solo.

In a very realistic fashion, the movie then unfolds with Ebba trying myriad methods to get her husband to own up to his selfishness. She's miffed. She's hurt. She prods. She's distant. And she habitually recounts the situation with unsuspecting friends and strangers.

Watching, I'm actively coaching, "Oh, come on, Tomas. Admit it." He on the other hand, will not concede. The family getaway is now tainted with tension.

Sound familiar?

Here's my point: All the guy had to do was see and admit his fault, then get on with Swiss skiing. But no. He just *could not* or *would not* get honest about what he had done.

Some Hard Experiences

I understand why it can be difficult—for some, *extremely* difficult—to be alive, even as a Christian. Sadly, I understand why it can be especially hard to live out your core calling to life and glory in the context of the Church. I, like you, have struggled in the context of church community.

Abuse

My father was abusive in every way. He verbally belittled my mother and older sister. Emotionally and spiritually, he regularly tried to confuse them and chip away at their confidence. He was physically abusive too. I recall shuddering at the kitchen table, while watching him bash down the bathroom door to get to my mom, then drag her out by her hair. He'd do all of this and then get up and preach on a Sunday morning.

As a local pastor, he brought a homeless man in one night and demanded my sister share her bed with him. Twisting Jesus' command to care for the poor, his cruelty wielded guilt and control on my teenage sister, "Share your bed. What kind of Christian are you?"

What an abuse of power and Scripture.

When he finally walked out on our family, frankly, mom was relieved. She would now raise her three girls on her own. I was five. It wasn't ideal, but in this case, it was better than the alternative.

Being A Woman

I've struggled as a woman in the Church. I've been told that my gifts of leadership and speaking can only be used in certain capacities because I am a woman. "You'll never be able to lead worship here. You're a woman," I was candidly told several years ago. I've always celebrated being a woman! I've been an active leader in the Church since I was a teenager. But in recent years the harsh realities of what I've faced as a woman have doused me with cold water. I've been awakened to the predicament of Christian women everywhere with far less support and voice than I.

Betrayal

A few years ago we discovered that a long-time volunteer youth worker who'd been "ministering" to our sons for years was in fact a sexual predator. We worked with police for months to gather the evidence to put him in prison where he now sits for a minimum of twelve years. He'd made his way into our family then preyed on our one son for five years.

I know what it's like to be hurt by the Church. I understand how easy it could be to throw in the towel. To shrink back. To get cynical or worse.

Heart Attacks

Christian or not, no one gets through this life unscathed. Jesus said, *"In this world you will have trouble. But take heart! I have overcome the world"* (John 16:33). He's speaking of the order of the Universe as we know it.[32] And when your pain comes at the hands of those who profess to love and follow Christ, the wounds are more severe.

Philadelphia pastor Dharius Daniels says, "We've suffered heart attacks."[33] So true. Our heart, this "wellspring of life," tender and open, where love of God and others flows, has taken its hits.

How honest can you be about *why* you tend to camp out where you do? Can you be honest about why you are where you are, and feel the way you do about God, yourself, and the Church? And how are you at seeing where you've contributed to the issues?

Issues in the Church

Here are just a few issues for us in the Church to get honest about.

Politics

I'm not spending much time here. If you're tuned into the news, you see it for yourself.

The Church got into bed with politics, and we liked it. In some ways, we can trace that all the way back to the Roman Emperor Constantine around 300AD. (There are flip sides to everything.)

Today, the Church in America is divided more than ever over politics. I know beautiful followers of Christ, including leaders and discerning Millennials who chose to get off social media because of the online cesspool among Christians over politics. We're clinging to our "rag rights" when rioting on social media.

Social Justice

We're hot about politics but have little fervor around blatant and systemic racism in our communities. In your church or Christian college, how often do you work through the issues of racism? Look at your friend group. As internationals, including refugees, come to our nations, is there room in your circles for "difference"? If you're a leader, what's the complexion of your leadership team?

What about the poor? The Bible has over five thousand references to the poor (Shane Claiborne, *The Simple Way*). Here's just one, but it's a doozy: *"Rich people who see a brother or sister in need, yet close their hearts against them, cannot claim that they love God"* (1 John 3:17). Ouch.

Do we take this seriously enough to forfeit time in Bible class to make room to actually live it out in your nearest homeless shelter?

These and other social justice issues are paramount to God. Rather than spend time deciding who's in and who's out, or split hairs over eschatology (how the end times will *actually* unfold), might we make them a priority in our own lives?

Singles

How have you experienced being a single woman in the church? I believe we've done a real disservice to single women. Whether you've never been married, you're divorced, or a widow, I fear we've perpetuated a message of second-class citizenship.

Cam and I always said to our boys, "*if* the Lord calls you to marriage," recognizing not everyone is called to this sacred human union. It's a very high calling. And so is singleness and celibacy. (An ideal commonly and unfortunately mocked in our culture.)

The pressures to marry ignore singleness, as an important part of Scripture as modeled by Jesus and the apostle Paul.

Paul's remark in first 1 Corinthians 7:8, "*if you are weak* (must have sex) *get married*" is very appropriate today.

Singleness is an equally viable lifestyle to God. Paul wrote that it's better to stay single for the sake of the Gospel. Single people can channel time, energy, and attention into God's calling over their lives. All for the sake of His kingdom!

Of course, whole cultures and societies are made up of the family unit and the "be fruitful and multiply" mandate. And certainly marriage is a God-ordained union and sacrament. It is the model of Christ and His Bride, the Church. But not everyone gets married. It's not for everyone. Maybe as a single woman, you've been disheartened.

Sexual Abuse and Infidelity

Every time I learn of a leader in the Church who turns out to be a sexual predator, I go silent. *No, God,* I pray. Another predator priest. But of course sexual abuse is not a Catholic issue. It's a Church-wide issue. It's a very real stronghold everywhere, but noticeably in the Church.

We know we're going to have trouble, but it's so much worse when it comes through the people of God, isn't it?

I understand being disappointed with the Church. I understand being excruciatingly frustrated with lies, betrayal, and a lack of Christ-likeness. If you're sick of hypocrisy, judgmentalism, and politics, you should be!

So was Jesus.

Jesus' Woes

While in seminary I did an analysis of all the opposition to Jesus and His ministry.

By far, Satan's most common agent was the religious. Especially the leaders.

Jesus warned: *"Now then, you Pharisees* (the Truth Protectors of the day), *clean the outside of the cup and dish, but inside you are full of greed and wickedness. You foolish people!"* (Luke 11:39-40).

"Woe to you Pharisees, because you give God a tenth of your mint, rue and all other kinds of garden herbs, but you neglect justice and the love of God. You should have practiced the latter without leaving the former undone" (Luke 11:42).

"Woe to you Pharisees, because you love the most important seats in the synagogues and respectful greetings in the marketplaces" (Luke 11:43).

"'And you experts in the law, woe to you, because you load people down with burdens they can hardly carry, and you yourselves will not lift one finger to help them" (Luke 11:46).

"Woe to you experts in the law, because you have taken away the key to knowledge. You yourselves have not entered, and you have hindered those who were entering" (Luke 11:52).

Many followers of Christ are desperately trying to live out Jesus' constant call to life even in the face of all this. But, it's tough.

Lord, Save Us From Your Followers

The documentary *Lord, Save Us from Your Followers* shows Christians pitching a confession booth at a large, open-air, gay pride gathering.[34] When tentative but curious LGBTQ + or their supporters entered the booth, they were met with a Christian.

But the unexpected happened. Instead of offering the LGBTQ + person an opportunity to confess and turn away from their life of sin, the caring Christian confessed *to them.*

"On behalf of the Church, we acknowledge and confess our lack of love, our hypocrisy, our pride and hatred," they said.

Those who experienced the pain of judgment at the hands of Christians were surprised and softened.

I've similarly apologized when I've had non-Christians in my home for specific outreach gatherings. (No bait and switch is used. Our friends are aware it's an exposure to Christianity kinda' gathering.) But I can tell you firsthand, that simply getting honest with non-Christians about where the people of God have failed, *where I have failed*, goes a long way in building bridges back to those we've desperately hurt.

Quit Defending

How many times have you felt the need to defend the Church? Honestly, it's not like you have to argue about this, we all know we've done a lot of stupid things. We've all wasted valuable time and energy defending, explaining, justifying, and denying. Anything but facing what's true.

We are the Church.

We've all hurt and been hurt by the Church. I have been too political. I have been too judgmental and hypocritical. I, like Tomas, am just that selfish.

Conclusion

We need to get honest about these things. We must. If we don't, like Ebba toward Tomas after the avalanche incident, we'll be miffed and hurt, prodding and distant. We'll "habitually recount the situation with unsuspecting friends and strangers." Especially people wondering about or wandering from God. Or we'll just walk away.

But, I promise you, if we own the sadness—not wallowing in it, but owning it—the Truth and Life that God calls us to in the midst of the sadness, and well beyond, will gush like water breaking through a dam!

We'll stop defending and denying. We'll stop blaming. Life will come from a deep sense of what truly *is*, without spiritually bypassing feelings, and the reality that we live in a world, and a Church that's muddled and messy.

In the next chapter, we'll look at what happens when we take what we've identified back to the place of hope.

In the meantime, thank you for being honest. And if you've been burned by the Church . . .

I'm so incredibly sorry.

———————————— ··•●●●●··· ————————————

Questions:

1. Share the wonderful things you've experienced through the Church.

2. How have you been hurt by the Church? (Don't bash the Bride. But do give space for people to share their stories and pain.)

3. In what ways do you think this experience has shaped where you tend to camp?

4. Confess a time you hurt the Church.

———————————— ··•●●●●··· ————————————

CHAPTER 14

Curses

"Death is not optional. Life is optional. Will you choose to live?"
—*Christine Caine*

Big Dreams. Rude Awakenings.

Early on in my marriage to Cam I had an impressionable moment. Sitting in a McDonalds's one day, boys happily playing in the ball room, I glanced over a nearby table and saw an elderly man and woman. They looked as though they'd been married sixty years.

The woman's worn eyes rolled and fluttered, eyebrows raised and head shook while she talked on and on. Nonstop. The man's head, tilted downward, was slightly turned away. He was hunched over and checked out. A shell of himself. It looked like he'd spent years being beaten down, years avoidant and unengaged.

Maybe I had the picture all wrong. Maybe it was just a bad first date. But today after twenty-nine years of marriage to Cam, I still haven't forgotten that image. I remember thinking, *there it is. In our marriages or in any relationship for that matter, we can curse or we can bless. We can crush down or we can lift up. We get to choose. Life or death.*

For the sake of the husband God entrusted to me, and the glory of

God in our marriage, that day I committed to making it a habit of choosing life.

Curses

We don't talk a lot about curses today in American culture. The term has been co-opted as a synonym for swearing ("Don't curse") or as a device in Hollywood movies. Images of witchcraft and the demonic come to mind. Long, bony fingers and crackling voices, "I curse you!" Most of us are not that up on the topic of curses.

As I speak in various countries around the world, I can tell you, cultures with voodoo roots present issues of deep-seated curses that most North American Christians know little about. Christians in these nations take curses very seriously.

Just like in biblical times.

Raca

Jesus warned, *"You've heard it said, do not murder, but I tell you, if you get angry, if you say, 'raca,' you fool, you're in great danger"* (Matthew 5:22).

Why? Because *raca* was a term that meant, "idiot." It pronounced "stupidity, inferiority, and foolishness" over a person. Cursing them.

Your twelve-year-old daughter has this down pat. Eyes rolling. Hand on hip. Furrowed brow. Without words, she's said it all.

So in true Jesus fashion, He takes things that were common in Jewish culture (the standard of the Law) and raises the bar. *"You've heard it said, do not murder."* You bet they had. The first century hearers of these words knew the Law well. *We don't kill people. Got it.*

But here, as in several other areas of life—adultery, tithing (gifts and offerings to God), handling enemies, to name a few—Jesus raised the bar.

". . . but I tell you if you get angry, if you say, 'raca' . . ."

He ties murder to angry name calling because of the spirit or intention behind the word, which ultimately murders the soul. Curses make pronouncements, unleash lies and ill will over people. This chips away at life. And God takes your life very seriously.

These things latch onto us. Blatant lies or worse—veiled ones. They cling to us, and can bind themselves to us. They have a way of working themselves into our souls and taking root.

Do these sound familiar?

- "You're just like your father." Said with disgust.
- "Who do you think you are?"
- "Spit it out! You're so careful."
- "You're a woman."
- "Don't run, you may fall."
- "I'm very disappointed in you. I expected more."

Like your twelve-year-old with attitude, sometimes words aren't even spoken. You just get the look, the turned back, or silence. It's the spirit of the curse that lets you know, *you haven't measured up.*

Nothing But Trouble

A frustrated mother flying alone with two preteen boys stood in the airport coffee shop juggling her own luggage and food for the family, all while trying to pay the barista. Neither boy offered to help—their noses were stuck in their phones. When the mom inevitably dropped one of the drinks she was balancing, she lashed out at the boys. "You were both so helpful when you were little. Now you're so selfish! You're nothing but trouble to me." Then she was silent. The boys looked away in shame.

Were the boys trouble? Selfish? Perhaps, sometimes. But trouble does not define them. Selfishness does not define them. That was just their mother's momentary burst of anger and frustration talking. But it was also a curse. A curse is a declaration of death. It's a declaration absent of love. And we've all done it.

Dealing with Curses

Here are suggestions in dealing with curses:

1. Identify Words. Think about words spoken over your life. This can be really difficult because you may feel like you're being disloyal to someone you love deeply. A mother. A worship leader. A priest. A spouse. A sister.

    Unintentionally, unconsciously, lies and attachments get woven into our identity.

    They've been spoken over us, and we've sometimes done it to ourselves. "I'm such an moron!" seems harmless. It's not. Contempt and condemnation loiter in those words. It's an agreement with an enemy who wants you lifeless: *Yes, you are a moron. You did it again, loser.*

    Take some time and journal (even point form) any words spoken over you. Be brave. Be honest.

2. Identify Actions. I've focused on messages spoken and unspoken, but of course stories abound in things actually *done to us.*

    I've spent years ministering to women. From wealthy and highly accomplished, to my dear sisters in the homeless shelter, from women across the globe, to women across the café table, non-Christian and Christian alike, every woman has a story.

    Sit with God and write down (in that same journal) painful actions that have affected your life. Have you been abandoned? Rejected? Abused?

    Counseling: In some cases I strongly suggest that along with working through these issues in this book, you may need to seek professional counseling (on your own or in a group). Ask someone you trust to make a solid suggestion.

3. Look at Jesus.

    "Christ redeemed us from the curse of the law by becoming a curse for us, for it is written: 'Cursed is everyone who is hung on a tree'" (Galatians 3:13).

We live in a sin-sick world. But Jesus absorbed and endured the cosmic curse (the fall), and our particular curses (sins against me, and sins by me) on the cross. (Remember the Cross Chart.)

When my kids were little, as they slept, I'd put my hands on their backs and talk to God about them: "Father, in Jesus' name, uproot any harm done through actions or words of discouragement, untruth, hostility that have come to David or Aaron today. From a well-intentioned Sunday school teacher, a harsh coach, or a bully. Lift these things off them, I pray."

As God brings to mind the harmful words spoken over you, or stories that have cut you down and chipped away at your life, pray. Because *"the prayer of a righteous person is powerful and effective"* (James 5:16).

Don't doubt it.

The example of how I've always prayed for my two sons is exactly how God sees us, His children. He loves us. Deeply loves us. We're working with Him to deal with curses that suck the life right out of us. Some of these issues are entrenched because they go back generations. Believe me, you can pass them down or shut them down. Cooperate with God to shut them down!

The cosmic curse of sin and death, and its effects in everyday life are the realities of living in a sin-sick world. We join Jesus in putting the powerful work of the cross into practice.

Deep Dives Not Always Necessary

If you've never done work like this with God, it may seem so unwieldy at first. Like cleaning out a storage closet. *Ugh, don't make me go in there.* And it is messy while you sift and purge. But eventually you see the results.

Periodically throughout our lives we'll do these "deep dives" but not all the time. That would be exhausting. It would also be living in the light of the bad news, with too much focus on the curse.

Ideally, you'll get to the place where in normal everyday living (like my earlier example of my adulterous thought while choosing cheese), you'll:

- Acknowledge these curses as they come—those placed on you and those you've placed on others, then . . .
- Deal with them early and often. (See chapter 11, "The Power of the Cross.")

Now look at that Galatians passage again and watch what happens next.

The Exchange

"Christ redeemed us from the curse of the law by becoming a curse for us, for it is written: 'Cursed is everyone who is hung on a tree.'

He did this in order that the blessing through Abraham might come to us through Christ" (Galatians 3:13,14).

Jesus absorbed and endured the cosmic curse and our particular curses, and in the cross he exchanged our curses for blessing.

CHAPTER 15

Blessings

"I make it my rule, to lay hold of light and embrace it, wherever I see it, though held forth by a child or an enemy." —Jonathan Edwards

Bless You!

We use explicit language of blessing a lot.

Send-offs, sign offs and knee-jerk responses to a sneeze: "God bless you!"

The language is far more common and familiar to us. It has an upbeat optimism that's not only perky (though a bit "churchy" at times), but carries weight in its original meaning and use.

To Bless

In the Scriptures, the language of blessing is used in gifts (blessings), and praise and thanksgiving, for example, *"I will bless the Lord at all times; His praise shall continually be in my mouth"* (Psalm 34:1).

It was common in biblical times for the patriarch to bless, or pronounce favor, prosperity or a prophetic word over his family. The aged patriarch Jacob, for example, blessed Joseph's sons in Genesis chapter forty-eight. As was tradition, his hands on their heads, he then made his patriarchal pronouncement or blessing over his descendants.

Leaders in the contemporary Church bless by bestowing favor, approval, and protection in the sacraments of marriage, infant dedication or baptism, and ordination to ministry.

A Mother's Blessing

In 2013, I sat at my beloved mom's bedside in the hospital.

Two weeks earlier, our whole family had celebrated her eightieth birthday in Toronto. At eighty she was beautiful, vibrant, and healthy. At one point during the party while people were "blessing her" with stories of how she'd impacted their lives, I distinctly remember thinking, *I'm so glad we're doing this. It seems a shame people wait til funerals to say these kinds of things en masse.*

A week after the party, a gallstone triggered a quick downward spiral of her health.

I arrived at the hospital in Barrie, Ontario, from Philadelphia right after submitting a seminary exam.

Once mom knew she was saying good-bye, she asked to speak privately with each of her three girls.

Mom's words to me were memorable and precious. Like the ancients, she blessed her children.

The most important and poignant for me was this: "Nancy, do you remember when you were a little girl on the bed?"

We held hands and locked eyes. I knew exactly what she was referring to.

On The Bed

When I was a child, after church on Sunday evenings (two or more services on a Sunday was standard for us), mom, Karen, Debra, and I would all climb up on Mom's bed and I'd reenact parts of the service.

My arm raised like a passionate, seasoned preacher, I'd lead us all in singing my favorite, "Heaven Came Down and Glory Filled My Soul!" We'd take turns choosing upbeat hymns. And I'd lead them. Then I'd ham it up and preach a "sermon." They cheered me on, amused by the boisterous baby of the family.

"Yes, Mom. Of course I remember."

"Honey, you had that little hand in the air. You had such fire, such passion . . . Do it. Move out. Preach Jesus. Give it your all. This—*this* is what you were made for," she affirmed.

And right there, just hours before the doctor removed all life support, I received the blessing of my beautiful mother to move into my calling as a Christian speaker.

My mind often drifts to the very clear blessing she spoke over my life that day.

Blessing is telling and supporting the truth. It does *everything* to call it out.

Telling the Truth

The woman who said her kids were only trouble wasn't only cursing her boys, she was lying to them. They're not *only* trouble. They may be some trouble—aren't we all? Her words were simply untrue.

We align ourselves with God when we seek truth. When we speak and live in truth.

At the end of his life, John (Jesus' disciple and closest friend), wrote: *"To the lady chosen by God and to her children, whom I love in the truth—and not I only but also all who know the truth—because of the truth, which lives in us and will be with us forever"* (2 John 1:1).

The "truth" John spoke of is the Good News of God's boundless love, demonstrated through Christ. The Gospel. This isn't hearsay with John, it's firsthand experience of Jesus' life, death, and resurrection. But not only that, John's reference here is to truth in the sense of things being, "as they really are." Layered into this is the very nature of God, who is Truth. That's three layers of truth.

- The Good News
- Things as they really are, and . . .
- Jesus, who says, *I am Truth*. Truth is a Someone. Jesus doesn't just tell the truth, or dispense truth, He is Truth. (Read the passage

again and substitute "Christ" for the words "the truth" and you'll see what I mean.)

There's no genuine blessing without truth. When we align ourselves with what's actually true, we align ourselves with God.

What's The Truth, Jesus?

A friend told me the story of a woman, let's call her Jenna, who struggled all her life with a spirit of rejection. As a grown woman, if she wasn't included in a dinner party, she was extremely hurt and offended. When she checked social media, if she saw her friends getting together without her she would spend the rest of the day really bugged by it. The slightest things would trigger her and she'd feel left out, down, and angry. It could destroy her whole day.

Through counseling and prayer, she was guided back to the day she first felt rejected. She had walked into a room where some family members—dad, mom, siblings, aunts—had been talking. She was almost five. When she entered, they all stopped talking. They looked at her.

"There," she remembered. She felt her tummy churn and tighten. Feelings of rejection and exclusion flooded back to her. She felt left out.

The wise counselor then prayed with Jenna, "God, what's the truth about that moment?"

Jenna and the counselor quietly sat waiting for God to lead them.

With the incident still in her mind, God revealed to Jenna what actually happened that day, all those years ago.

The day after the family incident that began this feeling of rejection was Jenna's fifth birthday. Her family threw a big party with balloons, chocolate cake, and hugs and kisses from family all around. A celebration of five-year-old Jenna!

Now with the counselor, thirty-six-year-old Jenna just sobbed. Rejection had implanted itself in her five-year-old mind and heart, but what was true was quite the opposite. She was not only accepted that day. She was loved and celebrated. What she perceived as rejection, in reality was not. It was restraint—they'd been trying to surprise her.

Bless yourself and others by telling the truth. Align yourself with God's blessing over your life. Go after it. And call it out.

Calling it Out

"Come out, come out wherever you are!"

Say that out loud. Try it. I can't say that without shouting in a kid-like voice. The words have a lilt that skip along like the child who once broadcasted them to hiding kids within earshot.

We join God in fulfilling His mission when we call out truth and glory anywhere we see them. We jump right into that Genesis 3 scene, "Where are you?" right along with God. Like a child parroting her parent's words, we join Him: "Where are you?" We're now on the lookout for all signs of Life, and calling them forth.

People who work with executives, performers, athletes, any expert in their field, know this: Capitalize on your strengths. Everybody's got them. Value and nurture them. Know your strengths and move toward them. Acknowledge your weaknesses, but capitalize on your strengths. Think of our four camps. Look at the diversity of strengths:

- The gatekeeping and quest for knowledge of the Truth Protectors.
- The grace and transparency of our Keepin' It Reals.
- The expectant belief of our #Blessed.
- And the humility and insight of our Untapped.

Strengths properly applied.

The Church is not like Pringles chips, lined up nicely in a row. We honor the diversity of our strengths. We call out the Imago Dei (image of God) in every human being God places right in front of your face.

What Does This Look Like?

Liberally and literally bless by calling out glory everywhere you see it.

- In our kids: "Ethan, I saw you. I heard you. That was bang on, buddy! God's giving you insight that's pretty amazing, honey." You step back from those kids at various points over the years and say, "Wow! Look at you. Look what God is doing in your life." I'm not talking about making kids into praise junkies. It's simply telling the truth and blessing the socks right off them!

- In the elderly: "I only pray that I will be as gracious and elegant as you are someday, Janet." Or "Tell us the story again about how you mortgaged your home for our church building."

- In the disabled: I have a friend named Bethanne. She's been dying of ALS for over a decade. A once outwardly vibrant woman, she's now a prisoner in her atrophied body. Regularly we say to these precious ones, "I know there's so much in there, beautiful woman. You have so much to tell. You are not alone." Deliberately make sure the disabled are aware, "I see you. You matter. You're alive and we call that out."

- In Denominations or Religions: It's a given we won't agree on everything. But look for where we do agree. "Wait, that made sense. That's good. I hadn't thought of it that way, but that really makes sense to me." Call it out whenever and wherever you catch a glimpse of truth. Bless them by calling it out.

You do this in everything from the profound to the seemingly frivolous. For young and old. Rich and poor. Black and white. Man and woman. *Everyone.*

If you consider yourself a strong, seasoned Christian, stretch yourself. Call out life where you'd really rather not.

Sin or Preference

Next time you find yourself turning your nose up at a person or people group, try this instead: *God, I see this coming up in me, help me to move toward this (liberal Democrat, Trump-loving Republican, tattooed, classy . . .) woman with a blessing.* Ask questions. Lean in and look for bridges to bless.

What we once found highly offensive, we may discover has more to do with our preferences and biases, not actual sin. Sometimes what we found highly offensive doesn't fly in the face of God's glory, but is another expression of it.

Blessings and curses are really about life and death. And at every point we get to choose.

Let's go back to the cross again to illustrate the process of dealing with curses and pouring out blessing.

Little Resurrections

We don't avoid our stories of curses, we acknowledge them. We get honest about where we've been cursed. And acknowledge where we've cursed others. Godly sorrow will come. And we grieve. We grieve our racist remarks, our abuse of power, our exclusion of others . . . we grieve our sin-sickness.

But then remember: *"Christ redeemed us from the curse of the law by becoming a curse for us"* (Galatians 3:13).

And at the same time: *"I have been crucified with Christ . . ."* (Galatians 2:20). We join Christ in the pain of Gethsemane and Golgotha. He invites us to go with Him and know Him there.

A word of caution: Don't jump too quickly to resurrection and skip feeling the pain. The depth of your grief and the depth of your joy are directly related. If you grieve deeply, your love, power, and rising is so much greater. If you dampen the grief, the authentic joy and power of the resurrection will be just as dampened.

"I have been crucified with Christ and I no longer live [the dying], but Christ lives in me. The life I live in the body [the living] I live by faith in the one who loves me and gave himself for me" (Galatians 2:20).

Just like what actually happened on the cross over two thousand years ago, and now happens with each curse that surfaces—we exchange our curses for His blessing.

In our death, God breathes His resurrection power.

In Christ, we rise!

CHAPTER 16

Excellence

"We are made for larger ends than Earth can encompass. Oh, let us be true to our exalted destiny." —Catherine Booth

When I say, "excellence" what do you think about? A teacher from the past? "Excellent work!" A recent project you hit out the park? Does that word make you sit up straighter and get a glint in your eye?

Or do you get a knot in the pit of your stomach? Feel stressed or inadequate?

Well, what do you mean by excellence, Nancy? Great question.

Definition

Here are some definitions:

"The quality of being outstanding; extremely good, excelling, accomplished, the state or quality of being exceptionally good."[35]

Or as I once heard someone suggest: "Matching your practice with your potential."

A common phrase, which I used on QVC, is this, "The very best version of you."

Excellence is not about doing big things. It's about doing anything—big or little, in private or public—beautifully. With attention, love, and commitment.

Emerging Glory

I suggested the work of getting honest and dealing with curses in service of two primary goals:

Accepting what we are and are not, and—

Establishing our awareness of our increasing desire for a great and glorious God.

Both open doors to genuine life.

These stimulate you to call out the glory of God where you see it. The inspiration intensifies—rising and rising—until that upsurge has us expressing with the Psalmist, *"with my God I can scale a wall!"* (Psalm 18:29).

And there it is.

Excellence emerges.

What Are You Eating?

I had a voice teacher who tapped into a deeper part of me as a singer when he experienced a less than inspiring rendition of an aria during a lesson one day. He's a passionate Puerto Rican! I'm passionate too, but apparently not that day.

He looked up at me from the piano and said with a gleam in his eye, "Nancy, what's your favorite meal?"

I didn't miss a beat. "Prime rib beef and Yorkshire pudding."

"Mmm . . . sounds delicious. Picture it right before you. Eat it. Devour it. *Now* sing the aria!"

I threw my arms open wide, imagined the crusted, rubbed roast with its drippings, drizzling down the puffy, delicious Yorkshire.

Then, deeply delighted (and amused), sang the aria. What a difference it made!

Unbeknownst to him, my voice coach tapped into God's core calling—where are you?—and took my singing to a whole new level.

That's what we want. But on a much higher level, we want to open our deepest selves to the Source of all that is excellent.

And it's not the roast beef, my friend.

Irresistible!

"LORD, our LORD how majestic (impressive, grand, regal) *is your name in all the earth! You have set your glory in the heavens"* (Psalm 8:1).

God's name is synonymous with His essence, His very core. And the essence of who He is spills into all He does. God is superior, perfectly excellent. This is known by us by what He does.

We don't say, "I'm an excellent employee just because of who I am. Of course I'm always late and cut corners on my work, but . . ." Who you are is only evident in what you do.

What you do reflects who you are, and who you are reflects what you do. As it is with God.

God Is Excellent

Everything about God—who He is what He does—is excellent and praiseworthy. Not a thing about Him is shoddy or average.

The Psalmist goes on:

"When I consider your heavens,
the work of your fingers,
the moon and the stars,
which you have set in place,
what is mankind that you are mindful of them,
human beings that you care for them?

You have made them a little lower than the angels
and crowned them with glory and honor.
You made them rulers over the works of your hands;
you put everything under their feet:

all flocks and herds,
and the animals of the wild,
the birds in the sky,
and the fish in the sea,
all that swim the paths of the seas.

"LORD, our Lord,
how majestic is your name in all the earth!" (Psalm 8: 3-9).

There's a pattern in here worth noting:

a)   God is excellent. *"LORD, how majestic is your name."*

b)   All He does—creating and sustaining—is excellent.
"When I consider your heavens, the work of your fingers . . ."
"You have made them (humanity) *a little lower than the angels and crowned them with glory and honor. You made them rulers over the works of your hands; you put everything under their feet . . ."*

c)   When you experience the majesty of God through His creation, especially humanity in all their glory as they live and care for creation, glory erupts through the praise.
"LORD, our Lord, how majestic is your name . . ."
Expressing God's magnificence fuels all we are!

You are high caliber. Masterfully engineered. Glorious. Do you see the permission and invitation, to bring your A game to your life?

God then rewards it.

Rewards

"Whatever you do, work at it with all your heart, as working for the Lord, not for human masters, since you know that you will receive an inheritance from the Lord as a reward. It is the Lord Christ you are serving" (Colossians 3:23, 24).

God loves to reward our gutsy, superior work.

"Living among the Babylonians, Daniel was exceptional and the king put him over all his kingdom" (Daniel 6:3).

The wisdom literature reminds us, *"Do you see someone skilled in their work? They will serve before kings; they will not serve before obscure men"* (Proverbs 22:29).

Jesus' telling of the parable of the talents in Luke 25:14-30, not only emphasizes reward for excellent use of entrusted resources, but warns against wasting them. God is extravagant, but He's never wasteful.

Excellence originates from God, then demands a corresponding response. Not "demand" as a parent demands, "Get straight A's!" but like a magnetic force that draws you up, as in the lyric, *"demands* my soul, my life, my all"* ("When I Survey the Wondrous Cross").[36]

It's a cosmic high-five!

Excellence—your excellence—is the only option for us as followers of Christ.

Being Excellent

Here are some thoughts about kicking it up a notch in all you do:

- **Know and Do.** Think about what you do really well. Maybe it's talking. Fine. Talking it is. What else? Are you a sensitive listener, gaining access to the hardest-to-love type? Is it violin? Hair? Debating? Geology? If you're stumped, ask someone close to you. Then find something—paid or unpaid—and fit it into your life. Don't hold off. Doing that is equivalent to holding off on getting a new outfit until you've lost X amount of weight. Don't. Get at least one outfit (secondhand, Target, borrowed, or boutique) *as you are* today, then work forward knowing you're accepted and beautiful. Same with doing something you know you love and do well.
- **Perpetually Learn.** Continually learn and grow in that area. He's given you gifts—spiritual or otherwise. Don't always assume to be the expert. Ask questions and learn from the best you can find.

In person, YouTube, Google, books, wherever you can. Surround yourself with people who know more about things you're great at, and about things that complement you. Listen, watch, and learn. If, for example, you're a doctor and bedside manner isn't your thing, take a course or see a counselor, but don't accept inadequacy in such a critical role.

- **Over-deliver.** "God, you have been so generous with me. I will be generous in all I do today." Over-delivering on gifts of time, acts of love, attention to detail, etc. stand out to God and others. If you're a teacher, be the teacher everyone's trying to get for their kid!

- **Ditch Perfection.** Seems like the opposite of excellence. It's not. You've heard, "practice makes perfect." Well, I grew up with "perfect practice makes perfect." That's a lot of pressure. Perfection is not the goal. Aim high, practice (prepare the thing) til it won't go wrong. But it may. And when it does, breathe and move on. Ditching perfection will keep you more relaxed and ready to take risks.

- **Stay Focused.** Not rigid, but focused. "[Amy Carmichael's] great longing was to have a 'single eye' for the glory of God. Whatever might blur the vision God had given her of His work, whatever could distract or deceive or tempt other than to seek anything but the Lord Jesus Himself she tried to eliminate" (Elisabeth Elliot, *A Chance to Die: The Life and Legacy of Amy Carmichael*).[37] God is always the main focus. His glory will pour out of you if it is. He'll give you a vision for excellence that's truly out of this world. Now what are you actually going to do? "Just glorify God" is too global and nebulous a vision. You need to bring that lofty and spot-on desire down to the practicalities. Transfer it into the focused work God has given *to you.*

- **Edit and Say "No"** Focus, in my experience, requires this next step. Most summers I take large sheets of paper and draw out all I'm planning to do in the year. I divide my life this way: spiritual development, service, work, home, family, personal development. Then I list everything under those categories.

Take personal development: exercise, read, practice my singing. Stuff like that. Then I pray over all of it. "Lord, my calendar is yours. All that I am is yours. What would you have me remove, keep, or add on?" And I spend a good amount of time praying about that. Then I edit. Looking at my whole life, I can see if I'm spending too much time in any certain area at the sacrifice of another. This keeps me from over committing. It serves the vision. I'm far more able to say "no." Maybe your "Edit" and "Say No" looks a little different. Regardless of how you do it, remember that if you aren't planning your own calendar, it will be co-opted by everyone else.

- **Go Steady.** Any good runner knows, "Go at your pace." Everything bombarding us today wants us to push, push, push, faster, and faster. "Did you get my text?" Listen, nothing exquisite and high quality was slapped together. Excellence takes a rock solid foundation that's built one layer at a time. Don't trip over other people's demands for "now" at the sacrifice of top quality work. (Note: if you're the kind who goes s-l-o-w with everything, fine. If that's your best, know that and plan accordingly.)

I'm sure you can add your own tried-and-true approaches to my list. Because you know exactly what it's like to want excellence from yourself and others. Nobody likes a sloppy job.

Sloppy Seconds

Remember the last time you paid to have a job done and it was done sloppily? It's disappointing. You don't hire a speech therapist for your child and say, "Average is good enough." When your mechanic gets your car "almost fixed," do you say, "That's great!"

Now it must be said, sometimes you've got to say, "good enough." Not everything you do has to be to the utmost. You'll kill yourself. Trust me, I've tried. Relax on "lesser things" (what those lesser things are is up to you, your family, and God), and keep them in their place. But for the main things, give it your all. And consider this:

As you're rising and growing and becoming more excellent, how are you bringing this to the Church?

Excellence in the Church

God pulled together His people and called them "a holy priesthood" (1 Peter 2:5). Sounds official. And a bit intimidating. It simply means paid or not, clergy or lay, we're all in this together. We don't leave the work of the kingdom to the "ministers." We are the ministers. All of us are ministers of the Gospel, regardless of how we earn money. We roll up our sleeves and bring our best to the work of God.

If you notice you're quite fantastic everywhere *except* in your local congregation, ask yourself: why is that?

I'm Busy

You say, "I'm busy." We're all busy. So do something about that. Busy isn't the mark of excellence, it's the mark of the frenzied, groping for meaning and glory.

Author and Christian leader Richard Rohr, draws on Thomas Merton's wisdom and cautions, "People may spend their whole lives climbing the ladder of success only to find, once they reach the top, that the ladder is leaning against the wrong wall."[38]

Author and speaker Francis Chan echoes the appeal: "Our greatest fear should not be of failure, but of succeeding at things in life that don't really matter."[39]

Again, it's not about whether you work in the marketplace. A realtor, science professor, makeup artist, full-time caregiver, or a CEO—all can be ministers to the glory of God. It's about bringing all those well-honed gifts, experiences, and resources to the meeting of God's people.

If you're so busy, you're not bringing your gifts—let alone your A game—to the Church, there's something other than busy going on. You owe it to yourself at the very least, to figure it out. As when a marriage is in trouble and neither spouse picks up the phone to make the appointment with a counselor, it's not just about busy. There's resistance, driven by other things.

You Have Everything You Need

Excellence isn't about the brightest and best, otherwise, the disciples would never have been chosen. Neither would you or I. Excellence doesn't look like one thing. It's quiet and calm, loud and boisterous, and everything in between. It's about each one bringing *their* best to Him.

You lack nothing—nothing at all—to be the person of excellence and glory God has called you to be. He has provided everything you need. You say, "That's not true! I don't have support at home. I lack inspiration and confidence. I have no training or mentoring or skill." Again, you lack nothing to be the person of excellence and glory God has called *you* to be.

The truth is, excellence can be phenomenal. But it's also downright risky.

Part 3

THE STRUGGLE

"Our glory is hidden in our pain, if we allow God to bring the gift of himself in our experience of it." —Henri Nouwen

CHAPTER 17

It's Risky

"The horror of Hell is an echo of the infinite worth of God's glory." —John Piper[40]

The stakes are high when we speak of the glory of God.

To ignore the inherent risks is like skydiving without reviewing procedures and signing consent. So let's not ignore them. Let's talk about the risks and face them head on.

Stealing God's Glory

All this talk of humanity's glory can be thrilling. I've taught this material for years. I've watched facial expressions and postures shift in women who never really thought about their glory—women from all around the world who've never been given permission to be gloriously alive. Tears come. Hope rises. They pause in wonder, *Is this true for me?*

Then quickly on the heels of hope comes skepticism. The caution bells go off.

Oh, come on. Look around. This enthusiasm is great, but it's just not realistic. For many Christians, as the opposition rises, here's the "spiritual" defense: *careful. You're getting dangerously close to stealing God's glory.*

This is an age-old risk.

So we pull way back. Rather than get excited about glorifying God, we practice extremes of low expectations—of ourselves and others.

Being glorious is a constant tension. We really are glorious, and we still do grasp for what is rightfully His.

Grasp and Grope

When I was a new mother, I thought that if I worked really hard, read the right books, and stayed close to God, my kids would turn out just right. In fact, I remember hearing of a family where the teenage kids were using drugs and going off the rails. My first thought as a judgmental, young mom was: *wonder what the parents did wrong.*

Ouch! I'm embarrassed to admit it, but it's true.

A few years later, my boys were around seven and nine when I hopped in the backseat of a car one night to go out with some girlfriends. Woo hoo! Girls' night out!

We got talking about parenting and God. As we did, I began to see that the pressure I felt to get it all right meant that if my boys did turn out the way I'd hoped, I'd secretly take the credit. I'd been so careful about giving God the glory in other more obvious areas of my life.

That took me off guard. I hadn't even thought about that when it came to parenting David and Aaron.

Turns out, grasping and groping for glory is a genuine struggle in everything.

Biblical Tension

On the one hand we read, *"Do not think of yourself more highly than you ought"* (Romans 12:3). On the other hand, *"And we all, who with unveiled faces contemplate the Lord's glory, are being transformed into his image with ever-increasing glory"* (2 Corinthians 3:18).

Ok, don't shoot *more* highly than we ought. But knowing just *how* highly we ought to think of ourselves is a struggle.

Here's another one: *"I am the LORD; that is my name! I will not yield my glory to another or my praise to idols"* (Isaiah 42:8).

Here again, on the one hand God says, *"I will not give my glory to another,"* and on the other hand, as I've noted throughout, He embeds His glory in us. This paradox is uncomfortable. It's a predicament. Which is it?

Caring about both of these ideas shows your sensitivity to honoring God. That's giving Him glory. It shows you're engaged in the center of biblical tension. The reality is that our balance is off at any given moment. We'll never have it totally settled. This can be discouraging. But it also relieves the pressure and invites you to continue the ebb and flow of a real relationship with God. When you feel careful but unanxious concern that you want to get something right, you're in the sweet spot.

God's good with the tension and the risks. He's been at it a long time.

Risky for John the Baptist

"They came to John and said to him, 'Rabbi, that man who was with you on the other side of the Jordan—the one you testified about—look, he is baptizing, and everyone is going to him" (John 3:26).

The crowd was protecting their favorite and trying to stir up jealousy in John the Baptist. (Careful of this, Church.)

But John didn't fall for it. He knew his calling was to sound the trumpet, preparing the way for Jesus, so he said to them, *"A person can receive only what is given them from heaven. You yourself can testify that I said, 'I am not the Messiah but am sent ahead of him'"* (John 3:27-28).

Risky for the Angels

Notice how John the disciple (not the Baptist) described what happened when he was confronted by a message from the angel: *"Then the angel said to me,* (John) *'Write: Blessed are those who are invited to the wedding supper of the Lamb!' And he added, 'These are the true words of God.'*

"At this I (John) *fell at his feet to worship him. But he said to me, 'Do not do it! I am a fellow servant with you and with your brothers who hold to the testimony of Jesus. Worship God!'"* (Revelation 19:9, 10).

I love how God didn't delete certain things in Scripture. It's not perfectly neat. It's messy. John (led by the Spirit of God) actually tells us he got caught up in the message that gave him the impulse to worship the messenger.

This is a caution for us to not misplace our worship. "She's so amazing." "I always and only listen to her." "I'm addicted to him." Be aware of how you elevate messengers. It can be a crushing load.

Too Heavy

Think about the allure of stardom and celebrity. We love our American idols. But think of all the tragic stories of people who looked like they had it all, then their lives took a turn for the worse: Anthony Bourdain, Marilyn Monroe, Whitney Houston, Justin Bieber, Britney Spears, and countless others. Tabloids and TV shows that ask, "where are they now?" often capitalize on the tragedy of public figures who have fallen under too heavy a weight.

Star athletes and high achieving students have ended it all. "But why? They had everything," we say.

We were not created to bear the weight of worship. It's far too heavy a load. We think we want it, but that level of attention and glory is too much for humanity to handle. We crush under the weight of what rightfully belongs to God.

God Alone

If you're disillusioned by the failure of a pastor, a college chaplain you trusted immeasurably, or public Christian figures like heads of mega churches, thank God for His divine commitment to strip away your impulse to worship them.

And what about your kids? Your kids don't have what it takes to handle your worship. Neither does your husband. I thank God that Cam simply cannot reach the deepest part of me, despite our fantastic marriage of twenty-nine years. Sometimes it really hurts. Then I remember that place is reserved for God alone.

Every glorious human will disappoint you.

No one can measure up to idol worship. No one can stand under it either. Don't blame them for failing to be the object of your worship. It was never their place.

Horror of Hell

Stealing glory happens with misplaced worship and with grasping what doesn't belong to us. It also happens when you shrink back, failing to maximize His renown. In the words of author and speaker John Eldredge, "Your playing small, does not glorify God."[41]

Glory stealing is high risk for us. And for God. But if we step into the life God's called us to, it's horrifying to the evil one.

The enemy is at war with God for worship. His horror is for us to get this and link arms in full force. So he divides and conquers, whispering to each of us, "Careful, you're getting dangerously close . . ."

He condemns, "Who do you think you are being all glorious?" He wants to choke the life right out of us.

So maybe our initial response is to protect God's glory. But there are other factors at play.

Who, Me?

What could this Author of Life call me to? He's so risky, He's liable to require anything!

We're incredulous: "God's calling me to what? I can't. I can't do that!"

This call to Life can make your pits sweat and your knees tremble. So you may even pull back, arms folded in a huff. Singer Regina Spektor captures this fear:

"You hear them through the windows and the doors
Everybody's time has come
It's everybody's moment, except yours."[42]

The truth is, sometimes we fear living even more than we fear dying. Don't be surprised by the fear. It's normal. Everyone's afraid.

Out of fear, we hide behind others by blaming them:

"If men would just stop . . ."

"If my church would only . . ."

"I can't because you . . ."

"But my children still need . . ."

"If God would just bring a great . . ."

Do you really want to do that? Do you really want to put the blame on everyone else as an excuse for not really living?

It's scary to be all in:

"God, multiply your glory by spending all of me!"

"Lord, shift my perspective of genuine Life."

It's risky to put yourself out there on the edge of your comfort zone, potentially wiping out in front of everyone. It's a very vulnerable place.

It's risky, 'cause it's scary . . . and hard.

True and Hard

Here's a sobering thought from Oswald Chambers: "If it's true, now it's hard."[43]

Dealing with your junk and opening yourself up to real life is not for the faint of heart. Look how Jesus addressed this: Jesus said, *"Enter through the narrow gate. For wide is the gate and broad is the road that leads to destruction, and many enter through it. But small is the gate and narrow the road that leads to life, and only a few find it"* (Matthew 7:13,14).

Jesus was talking about entering eternal life. When we read "eternal life," we often think "heaven." But it's not only heaven. It's God who is Life. It's not about heaven later. It's about God inviting us into His unending (eternal), Life (Himself) now. Today and every day.

But, very few people—Christian or not—will deal with the stuff you've worked on in this book to really come alive. My prayer is that you'll be one of the courageous ones, entering the narrow gate. But I warn you: it's rare because it's hard. So you will stand out.

Tall Poppies

Picture rows and rows of uniform poppies in fields and gardens. They're all the same height, except for some who grow taller than the rest. The practice by those tending the tall poppies is to come along and *whop!* chop them down to size. "No tall poppies, we're keeping uniformity."

But what happens if God's created you to be a tall poppy? What do you do? What do you do when you really begin to live and do your thing? To stretch and grow and rise?

The Untapped are clenching their jaws about now. The idea of standing out is uncomfortable for them. But that reaction is not unique to the Church, though you can imagine how strong the urge can be to adopt this practice given the risks. Being a tall poppy, like taking the narrow road, is hard.

But God's willing to take the risks. He has since the beginning of time.

The question is not, do we try to steal God's glory? We do. It's in our nature. The question is how do we handle our desire to take what's not ours?

CHAPTER 18

Humility

"I am content to fill a little space if God be glorified." —*Susanna Wesley*

W hen speaking of excellence to the glory of God, the temptation of pride is inevitable.

Pride

Pride lurks, slithers, and coils around our toes, arches, and ankles. It's an attitude that whispers: *I deserve better. I deserve this.* Then, *I want this. I'll take this.*

Agreement by agreement. Justification by justification. Step by step. It tightens ever so slightly until . . . It. Pulls. You. Down. It's not like we weren't warned: *"Pride goes before destruction, a haughty spirit before a fall"* (Proverbs 16:18).

As one of my friends from QVC would say, "You can move from Hero to Zero like [snap] that."

The antidote to pride isn't fear and mediocrity. We actually diminish God's glory when we allow fear and mediocrity to set in. The enemy sows those things—they aren't from God.

The antidote to pride is humility.

The Antidote

Genuine confidence and excellence link arms with humility (notice "genuine"). Together they crush pride. True confidence, excellence, and humility are not oppositional. They're friends. But there is no *genuine* confidence and excellence without true humility.

Low

The Latin word for humility is *humilus*, which literally translates to "low."

Anjezë Gonxhe Bojaxhiu was a strong, small-framed, Albanian nun, who devoted her life to going low. She stooped in the streets of Calcutta to care for the poorest of poor.

Certain of God's call on her life, Anjeze, better known as Mother Teresa, humbly requested permission to leave her role as a teacher to spend the rest of her life loving the destitute in the streets. Submitting to Vatican authority, she waited patiently, uncertain of their cooperation. All the while, she prayerfully submitted to Christ: *As You will, Lord.*

God's will was accomplished. Mother Teresa relocated to a room, which she asked to be stripped of superfluous comforts so she could better relate to the people she was now called to serve.

She established The Missionaries of Charity that grew internationally and received the Nobel Peace Prize in 1979. Through years of media interest garnering global attention and awards, Mother Teresa humbly maintained, "I'm only a pencil in His hand."

Interestingly, when you fly into Albania's Tirana International Airport, you drive through Mother Teresa Square, which features an immense statue of the woman who spent her life going low. In accordance with the Scriptures, in some form or fashion, on earth or in heaven, by humbling ourselves, we are lifted up.

True humility is understanding that everything good that we do and have and are becoming is because of God. Every breath of that understanding points back to God in word and deed. Humility does not isolate from God and others with poor me-isms (Poor me, I'm not worthy. Poor me, I'm not good enough.) True humility drives us into relationship.

Self-Focus

Even if you don't do any of what I'm suggesting in this book and instead stay right where you are, you cannot avoid pride. *Here's what will keep me humble,* you may reason: *I'll keep confessing, over and over and over . . . keep reminding myself of my sin and desperation. Keep beating myself up. Keep hiding. That'll keep me humble. That will keep me from falling into destruction.*

If you never set your eyes where Christ is seated above, you'll be sitting in the seat of self-focus. The focus is still *your self.* Your interest is still you. Constantly ruminating on your fallenness is still self-centeredness. Self-absorption is delicious. We lap it up. We'll take the attention any way it comes.

This is a truth that C.S. Lewis picked up on and expressed this way, "True humility isn't thinking less of yourself. It's thinking of yourself less." True humility puts the attention where it belongs.

Yet, even as I write this, I'm sensitive to the realities of many women. When by God's grace, for example, you've pulled yourself out of family dysfunction or poverty, struggled to become clean, or get educated because you heard it was your ticket to a better life, humility is a fine theological idea, but seems highly impractical. I found that out while speaking to female leaders in Haiti.

Back To Haiti

At one point in the conference, I was sharing the testimony of my personal calling. The fact that I'd put my career aside to stay at home with children was not received well.

"Why would you do that?" some protested later. "Why go down when you're on your way up? No way! We've fought too hard." As a white, educated, married woman living in America, relatively speaking, it was easy for *me* to say this!

So for them, humility is perceived as, "keep taking the lesser positions." But I don't believe that's always the case. (Though it may be.) It means as you rise, keep that spirit charged with holy fire, humble.

If you've finally gained equality or at least a voice, praise God! And still remember, the way of Jesus is the way of humility. This essential is found precisely in this paradox: The way up is always down.

Why?

Because pride is insidious. The Untapped pride themselves in requiring little. Truth Protectors pride themselves in being right and good. Keepin' It Reals are proud they're not proud (and uptight) like Truth Protectors, and #Blessed may strut their stuff, what with all those blessings.

Humility does not come naturally. But humility is the antidote to pride.

So we come alive in Christ, pregnant with purpose, *"Humble yourselves, therefore, under God's mighty hand"* (1 Peter 5:6).

Humble Yourself

"And being found in appearance as a man, he (Jesus) *humbled himself by becoming obedient to death—even death on a cross! Therefore God exalted him ..."* (Philippians 2:8-9).

That was Jesus humbling Himself. Jesus. God incarnate modeling humility. Humbling ourselves doesn't usually involve a literal cross—how utterly humiliating, outrageously scandalous, and brutal that was for Jesus. But it does involve dying. A crucifying of pride. It takes regular humbling.

Taking his cue from Christ, the Apostle Peter wrote: *"Humble yourself therefore under God's mighty hand, that He may lift you up in due time"* (1 Peter 5:6).

Think about the metaphor of baptism used for over two thousand years, foreshadowing and then echoing what ultimately occurred on the cross. You are dying to live.

What precedes the lifting? The humbling.

As we hear God calling us to rise, let me suggest two things: 1. Practice humbling yourself, and 2. Embrace it when it comes.

Practice Humbling Yourself

Here are a few ways to practice humility:

- **Try not taking the best.** Practice taking parking spots, for example, that aren't the most convenient or closest to your destination. When you do, pray: "God, I don't always need the best. I trust that you give me everything I need and always will."

- **Fast.** When we speak of fasting, we commonly think of abstaining from food. But it really just means, going without. Do you fast? How often? From what?

  I once did a fashion fast. I wanted to see just how attached I was to style and beauty and all it brought in its train. So for three weeks I ditched makeup, stylish clothes (I only wore my garden jeans—simple and yes, clean; simple running shoes and a T-shirt). Seriously. No jewelry except my wedding ring. I was clean but not adorned. I paid attention to what came up in me as I went from place to place (including Saturday nights out and church on Sunday) in my fasting state. And I refrained from telling people what I was doing. Was it hard? At times. But it moved me toward knowing God and myself.

  Humility allows us to do without. A man spent some time at a monastery for some quiet reflection. The monk got him set up in the sparse, little room, then said before leaving the man alone, "Let us know if you need anything and we'll teach you how to live without it." Practice humility through fasting.

- **Be quiet.** Zip it. This is hard for verbal people like me. It's not just about giving space for others or respecting your friend or spouse by not finishing their sentences, it's about humbly being aware of God and others.

  Author Richard Foster said, "The only one safe to speak, is the one who is free to be silent" (Richard Foster, Good Samaritan Church conference).[44] Practice this.

- **Be kind.** The Gospel flattens cultural ranking. If you're in a position of power, that's a gift to be used to bring heaven to earth. I've seen Christians ruled by cultural norms, treating those in "lower positions" poorly. Take service providers for example. Housekeepers in the Philippines, the one who gives you a pedicure, a waiter in a restaurant—Jesus doesn't care what society dictates, His way is, "Treat people as you'd like to be treated." Mistreating people, being harsh and haughty is not the way of Christ.

- **Practice decoding:** Philip Smith was the Principal Trumpet of the New York Philharmonic orchestra from 1988-2014. He and I worked together for a week of music at a Salvation Army National Music camp several years ago. We had terrific discussions around the realities of being on stage as Christians. I never forgot what he shared with me: "It takes great confidence to get up on a stage and say, 'Here I am. I have something really good to share with you.' If you don't have that confidence, you can't do it. You won't be able to deliver. But once you step off that platform, step on that attitude that just may have crept in. Decode." After doing anything particularly public, pray, "God, now remove any pride that got on me during that time, anything that vies for attention and acclaim. I am your servant."

- **Ask questions.** Ask questions of people. This is a highly overlooked act of humility and love. Few people actually ask questions. It's remarkable. If you've already mastered the art of communication, which is like a tennis game back and forth ('cause keeping the ball's no fun!), the next level for you is to not just ask questions (a great behavioral demonstration of humility), but to take it to the next level with *actually being interested* in what another has to say without wondering, *when's my turn?* You may not get a turn in that conversation. Humbling, right?

- **Don't assume.** Avoid assuming because another differs politically, doctrinally, or culturally that they're foolish, unintelligent, or ungodly. See if you make assumptions about other denominations: "They speak in tongues!" or "They don't speak in tongues!"

   Think about how easy it is to make assumptions about the intelligence of those who don't speak our language. Do you know any internationals? (Maybe you are one.) Do you know what it takes to move to a nation and not speak the language? The rigor, stamina, courage, and humility it takes to uproot and leave what's known?

   Most of us don't. Most of us really struggle to humbly visit other nations and not demand American norms. "What do you mean you don't speak English?" Don't assume.

- **Lighten up.** If you can't laugh at yourself, that's too bad. We say and do funny things regularly.

   When we moved from Toronto to Nebraska, my university friends staged an intervention: "You can NOT move to Nebraska." Against their cautions we relocated from a great city to a cornfield in middle-America. When we moved from Nebraska to the Philadelphia area, Cam often introduced us as "the Hicks from Nebraska." I'd just smile. Don't take yourself too seriously.

- **Empty the trash.** Great leaders and mighty people of God living the abundant life aren't above emptying trash. (Or whatever your version of "emptying the trash" is.) If you're an up-front prominent person, practice taking a lowly position for humility's sake. I'm not talking about changing your job. (Although God may require that of you.) I'm saying, if you're the choice Bible teacher, go hold a baby in the nursery now and again. If you're in the limelight, do something where your name doesn't come anywhere close to the light. Do it. Squirm in anonymity. Practice getting messy and dirty.

- **Don't always be the expert.** Put yourself in positions where you're not the expert. If you find you steer clear of trying new things or jumping in when you're not the expert, rethink this. It could be a sign of pride. Periodically play games or sports you're not good at. Just for fun! If you're exceptional, now and again engage in discussion with, or simply listen to others who know far more on a particular subject matter than you do.

- **Read obituaries.** One of Cam's colleagues does this on a regular basis to remind himself, "I'm not above dying." Similarly, my son has spent time wandering among tombstones reading the epitaphs of those who've passed on. He says it's a great reminder and "totally humbling."

- **Receive a compliment graciously.** Really. God has seen fit to call and equip you to join Him. Humility means genuine gratitude for what God has done and for other's appreciation. Take the compliment graciously, and respond with a humble "Thank you."

- **Posture.** As you rise in your God-given glory, get on your face. Literally. Whether you're a "first lady" (pastor's wife in the African American church), a pastor, leader, rising role model, beautiful, rich, talented, have a PhD, are growing a ministry, whatever—get on your face.

  Anything God uses to raise you up can be the very thing that causes you to fall. Start out some mornings bowing down (if you're physically able). Use a phrase like, "I submit to your authority, God." Aligning your body and your soul goes a long way in reinforcing humility. It's a layered reminder: God, I confess, You rule, and everything good comes from you.

These practices, among others, prepare us for the times when humility, by God's kindness and mercy, just comes your way.

Embrace Humility When It Comes

We practice humility to mitigate and address pride. We practice humility to build a healthy base, so your knee-jerk reaction when life hits is steady and kind.

Because you and I both know, sometimes when things go seriously awry, despite God's work in you, pride rears its ugly head: *Who's in charge here? Somebody fix this!* we may demand. Breathe. Then thank Him that He loves you too much to let you get away with behaving like an undisciplined child.

Benin Bound

As I write this chapter, I'm sitting in Charles de Gaulle airport in Paris, France. And doesn't that sound lovely? It's not. I was en route to Benin, Africa, but my journey was halted yesterday.

I was invited to speak in Benin at a conference, train women leaders, preach, and as it is with most international speaking, be flexible to see what else God would inevitably open up. I was prayed up and prepared. So I thought.

I made the drive from Philadelphia to Washington to fly out of Dulles International. I boarded the plane to Paris.

Of course I barely slept on the plane, then had a four hour layover in Paris. About thirty minutes before boarding I went to the gate to check seating and air miles.

"May I see your visa please?" the lovely Parisian requested.

"Oui," I called upon my Canadian heritage.

After a couple of minutes, she looked at me and said, "Madame, this visa is not valid."

I got that feeling in the pit of my stomach. "What do you mean, not valid?"

Turns out that though the Benin embassy asked for my dates of travel to the country before they issued the required visa, they had in fact issued me a visa that didn't include my actual travel dates. A clerical error.

My head got light. I was queasy.

"What do we do?" I pleaded. "Is there anything I can do?"

God's Leading

Immediately I began to pray. "Lord, help me. What do you want me to do? Do I push through, or is this you rerouting me home? Lead me."

Short of hoping I could get another visa in time for the next flight to Benin later the next day, which I'd have had to pay for since I couldn't use my existing ticket, and praying I'd have the visa (if at all) before that next flight, it seemed clear, I was to turn back.

Frazzled, I sat down. I felt small and helpless, but strangely calm. And curious. I was mostly curious about God's leading. *I'm not leading this thing, you are, Abba,* I prayed.

And I was embarrassed. How could we have made this mistake? I remembered my visitation of the Truth Protector mentality that had reared its ugly head a couple months earlier. I'd seen a man at the airport in Philadelphia in the same situation. I remember thinking, *Poor man,* and I meant it. *But how could you make a mistake like that?*

I spent the rest of the day, tired and achy, navigating a massive airport to retrieve my luggage, and figuring out how to get home without it costing my first born. All the while I felt deeply sad and sorry for letting the church down in Benin.

God's Timing

When I finally got to my hotel (oh, yeah, I had to find one of those too), I lay on my bed, crying, "Lord, did I mess up? Should I have pushed through? If you didn't want me there, why not intervene earlier? Like before I bought the ticket or flew to France? That'd have been nice."

I don't always like God's timing.

His timing and clarity is sometimes confusing. Is this a yes, a no, a wait, or what? And sometimes when it seems it's a clear yes, things switch. God allows (or instigates) things to be turned around. And let's face it, as much as we listen and do our best to follow Him, sometimes it's confusing. It's so humbling to not be in charge.

Me Too

I'm starting my own "Me Too" movement around God being in charge of everything:

- You've been confused? Me too.
- You believed it was God and then weren't so sure? Me too.
- You've wondered, *What was that?* Me too.

I have a friend who was trying to adopt a child. She and her husband decided to take the plunge. They believed God had softened their hearts and united them as a family to "welcome the orphan." Very biblical. Surely it was God. Then it never happened. She cried with me over a cup of tea in my home late one afternoon, "I don't understand God. I thought it was a yes." I know. Me too.

It's all just so humbling, isn't it?

Holy Rascal

God is over all. Over every situation and circumstance, we—as indicated by things like death and weather and clerical errors—are not.

In all these situations, what I know is that I am not in charge. He is. He leads and promises, *"my sheep will hear my voice"* (John 20:27). No sense acting like Chief Shepherd when I'm a sheep.

I'm learning not to waste time wondering *why?* Or even, *what?* Better still, I'm learning to ask: "Who are you?" Because in it all, God is revealing Himself. For instance, when this Benin debacle happened, my friend Cheryl responded, "He's a rascal. A Holy Rascal." I recognized that as true! And I responded in kind, "God you're so big. So other. So unpredictable."

I won't let this truth about God make me extra cautious or fearful when He's lifting, and moving, and calling us to life. Instead, I'll get up and move with Him. Won't you join me?

CHAPTER 19

Suffering

"Now I rejoice in what I am suffering for you."
—The Apostle Paul (Colossians 1:24)

The resurrection of Jesus Christ that secured unending Life for all is built into the fabric of everyday living.

The cross is the pinnacle and symbol of this great paradox: death brings life.

Every time you see a cross, remember this: Death brings life. It's not what you or I would have chosen, but it is the way life works.

Death Brings Life

Do you work out? How hard do you push yourself? I work out at a local gym, and I've caught glimpses of seriously fit men and women. They're strong and chiseled. Above abrasive music, their trainers shout, "This is only temporary! Feel the burn," and "This is where the change happens!"

Suffering brings results.

Any woman who's ever given birth knows it too.

With each passing month, she watches her waistline expand and ankles swell. She's kicked and jabbed from the inside. She pukes.

Her skin's stretched and itchy. She's so pregnant!

On delivery day, everything hurts: Her back, her groin, her feelings and dignity. Her whole belly contracts causing excruciating pain.

She pushes to exhaustion, sensing things coming out of her that she'd rather have tucked back inside. Her body tears.

She pushes, and pushes until . . .

Birth.

New life.

Suffering is like that. Difficult. Dark. Long. Excruciating. And worth it.

The Body of Christ

Christ's body came through the birth canal. Christ's body was covered in slimy vernix and blood. It was laid in straw in an animal's feeding trough.

As a toddler, Christ's body tripped and skinned its knee.

It later grew faint from hunger and thirst, was scorched under the sizzling Middle Eastern sun, and was heavy with fatigue. Christ's body sweat. It stank.

Disgust psychology keeps us from talking like this. (Like mentioning that the tissue-thin seat covers in public restrooms don't actually protect you from the germs on the toilet seats. I don't want to know this!)

But it's true. Jesus was fully God and fully man. At the same time.

On what we call "Good" Friday, Christ's body was then beaten, slapped, spat on. It was whipped, pierced, and hung on a Roman cross.

Then placed in a tomb.

Three days later, after disarming the powers of hell and making a public spectacle of them, that body was raised to life! Glorified (Colossians 2:15).

Jesus suffered *and then* was glorified.

Another name for the Church is the Body of Christ. Today, in our suffering, we (the Church, Christ's Body) participate in revealing God's story of life and glory through our suffering.

Revealing Jesus

"Now I rejoice in what I am suffering for you, and I fill up in my flesh what

is still lacking in regard to Christ's affliction for the sake of his body, which is the Church" (Colossians 1:24).

When Paul, inspired by the Spirit of God, wrote these words to the Church in Colossae, he was in chains. Literally under arrest. His words are not trite and cliché. They're from a man who knew suffering and through it knew Christ. Intimately.

But what does, "fill up in my flesh what is still lacking in regard to Christ's afflictions" mean?

The work of Christ on the cross was finished work. There is nothing "lacking" in the perfect life, death, and resurrection of Christ. When Jesus uttered the words, "It is finished" from the cross, he didn't mean, "I'm dead, it's over." No. He was declaring: "mission accomplished!"

The work He came to do was complete (John 19:28, 30).

So what is still lacking?

This Is My Body Broken For You

Not everyone saw the summit (to date) of God's master plan. We weren't there that first Good Friday. All humanity didn't stand at the cross and actually witness the suffering and death of Christ.

But our suffering fills in, or "fills up" the gap.

Every bit of your suffering demonstrates Christ's passion. *The* Passion. (Passion literally means "to suffer." Those of us who are passionate get this.)

Our suffering today displays the crucifixion to everyone who did not personally witness the two thousand-year-old event.

What was, and is, still lacking is the present day revealing of this suffering that saves. That's our part. It's an individual suffering—Paul, you, and I—for the sake of the whole. For His Body.

It's out of this suffering that we present today *"the word of God in its fullness . . . Christ in you, the hope of glory"* (Colossians 1:25-27).

Word of God In Its Fullness

I wrote earlier that there's nothing more powerful, more exciting, and beautiful than the fullness of Christ, which is the Life of Jesus in His people, *His Body.*

That's right. And the fullness of Christ includes suffering. There's nothing more precious, more revealing of Jesus, than alive and present suffering that ultimately yields glory.

Suffering and glory are inseparable.

Together

The camps of Christians I've identified reveal the ever-present differences that rub against and ruffle feathers whenever we get up close. Any healthy family, couple, friendship, or close work relationship knows this.

There is no glorious Christian, apart from the glorious Church. The Church is always the collective. Always community. And together we suffer.

But apart, we're devoured.

Isolated Elephants

Cam and I celebrated our twenty-fifth wedding anniversary on African safari.

One of the days, instead of being out charging across the rugged terrain in the open jeep, we were on a trek.

The Botzwanese armed guide was clear: "smallest one in the middle." That meant me. I trekked along with five other larger, stronger men and women in front and behind me.

The hippos and lions we'd seen at a distance wouldn't think twice about carrying off and devouring the weakest one. A day earlier, I'd seen lions tearing into the meat of an isolated elephant. Waiting their turn, more lions lay under a nearby tree. Just over my shoulder, several more lions approached. They'd sniffed out the feeding.

Each of us is the weaker sister at some point. No exception. It doesn't matter how smart, resourceful, or godly. A storm wipes out the house. A husband leaves. A daughter hangs herself. In those moments, our knees buckle.

If you've become disillusioned with people who call themselves Christians, don't make the mistake of separating yourself. Yes, you'll suffer, but the alternative is so much worse.

Vulnerability and Compassion

How much more caring are we when a friend's mother dies, if we've lived the loss ourselves?

Suffering brings vulnerability that cultivates compassion like nothing else. It softens and strengthens us.

We're more patient today with parents who have troubled kids because we know what it's like to parent challenging ones of our own.

If you're stuck trying to figure out all the issues and mitigate suffering—and let's be honest, we all do to some extent—you can rest. Life and death are certainties.

If your desire has turned to a demand that the people of God be only excellent, only exemplary, only glorious, reconsider. For reasons you may never understand, their best may be you at your worst.

Our Suffering

Knowing our tendencies, our frustrations and differences, can we accept that these are inevitable, and are woven into the fabric of all life? Especially Church-life? Can we move toward each other in this holy death-yields-life struggle?

- The struggle of being misunderstood.
- The struggle of division.
- The struggle of being unknown.
- The struggle of blame.
- The struggle of loneliness.
- The struggle of fear.

- The struggle of power plays.

We long for the glorified Body of Christ, not the suffering one. But there is no glorified Body without suffering.

I know as you read this, you have questions. Of course you do. You've suffered. Maybe you're in a place of deep struggle and pain even now. But the Spirit of the suffering Savior, through Paul, who also suffered, urges us: *"I consider that our present sufferings are not worth comparing with the glory that will be revealed in us"* (Romans 8:18).

Part 4

ALL RISE

"God has given us eternal life, and this life is in his Son." —1 John 5:11

CHAPTER 20

The Glorious One

"May our tenure on this planet be characterized by one simple word: Jesus."
—*Beth Moore*[45]

All true magnificence, beauty, and glory come from God. All. No exceptions. The Good News is that right from the start, we have been designed for and immersed in this same glory.

How can we better realize this in our lives today?

We need vision.

Vision

I latched onto something I heard Dr. Larry Crabb say years ago: "Vision has more power to release the soul than insight has to change the soul."[46]

See, looking back on our lives, digging into what has influenced and shaped us is important. That's insight. But we don't want to build our houses there. It's necessary, but insufficient. Instead, looking *toward* something—having a vision—opens us up and moves us like nothing else. We are what we see. Our thoughts, feelings, choices, etc., have the potential to be drenched in the Source of all beauty and life.

Little Lucy Prevensie

In C.S. Lewis's *The Lion the Witch and the Wardrobe*, we meet a character I most relate to: Lucy Prevensie. She's the little, wide-eyed baby of the family who stumbles into Narnia, makes friends with all types of creatures, and runs back home to invite her siblings to join her. In the original series' second book, *Prince Caspian*, we find Lucy wandering out early in the morning to find Aslan the lion (the Christ figure in Lewis's books). Lucy walks along with Aslan, running her fingers through his mane, lies in meadow grasses, plays hide-and-seek and frolics with Him. I get Lucy. I am Lucy.

I Saw Jesus!

When I was about three, my family lived in western Canada. My parents were Salvation Army corps officers (Army speak for church pastors), and we lived in a house attached to our church. One evening, my mother was downstairs in the church holding a women's gathering. I had wandered out of my bedroom and was padding through the house in search of mom. Scuffing through the stairwell that joined the house and church, my chubby face tilted up as I detected something through a large window. It was Jesus.

Stop.

Today, can I tell you what He looked like? No. Can I tell you for sure that it was God? No. But that little three-year-old Nancy believed it was God. My exhilaration was unreasonable.

"I saw Jesus!" I squealed over and over.

Maybe it was my childish imagination—could've been a cloud. I suppose it might've just been an excuse I crafted so my mom wouldn't be mad at me for being out of bed. Who knows?

But maybe I really did see Jesus.

Here's what I know: I have always had a desire to see and know God. To find Him. Like little Lucy Prevensie, excitement has always bubbled up into persuading others to "Come see, come see!"

How Do We See God?

Most of us have never actually laid eyes on God, though God has revealed Himself in visions and dreams throughout history. Even today, reports and countless testimonies of Muslims, for example, coming to believe that Jesus is who He says He is, involved a vision or dream. Still, many of us have not had a literal "God sighting." So how do we see Him?

We start by asking God to open our eyes. Seriously. Let it be a daily prayer.

Then, as with humility, we practice. *Practice* seeing Him. Of the multitudes of ways of seeing God, here are three I find tremendously helpful:

1. Scripture. Knowing the Scriptures helps us know (again, *experience*, not just intellectual knowledge) and therefore see God. They tip us off to recognizing Him everywhere. Scripture's been inspired (breathed out) by the Holy Spirit whose job description includes revealing Jesus. The Holy Spirit also is working in the life of the reader, allowing the eyes of our hearts to "see."

You can see God in every passage of Scripture. In fact, all Scripture is primarily about God. But here are three examples of passages that help us see:

Old Testament

> "Praise the LORD, my soul.
> Lord my God, you are very great;
> You are clothed with splendor and majesty.
> The LORD wraps himself in light as with a garment;
> He stretches out the heavens like a tent
> And lays the beams of his upper chambers on their waters.
> He makes the clouds his chariot
> And rides on the wings of the wind.
> He makes winds his messengers,
> Flames of fire his servants"
> (Psalm 104:1-4).

The Psalms are filled with passages like this. They give us fantastic, poetic power in seeing God. Here's one from Isaiah:

"In the year that King Uzziah died I saw the LORD, high and exalted, seated on a throne; and the train of his robe filled the temple. Above him were seraphim. Each with six wings: with two wings they covered their faces, with two they covered their feet, and with two they were flying. And they were calling to one another:

> *'Holy, holy, holy is the LORD Almighty;*
> *the whole earth is full of his glory.'"*

(Isaiah 6:1-3).

One "holy" isn't enough as your vision increases. You'll find yourself echoing back the shout of the angels! Now to the final book of the Bible.

"Then I saw a Lamb, looking as if it had been slain, standing in the center of the throne, encircled by the four living creatures and the elders. He had seven horns and seven eyes, which are the seven spirits of God sent out into all the earth. He came and took the scroll from the right hand of him who sat on the throne. And when he had taken it, the four living creatures and the twenty-four elders fell down before the Lamb . . ." (Revelation 5: 6-8).

They're so visual! I feel swept up in the images portrayed. You can jot down one of these (or a favorite passage of your own) on an index card and pop it in your car or on your bathroom mirror. (Or near your journal and Bible.) Read it often. Visualize. Think about it. Ask God questions around it. "Lord, what does it mean that . . . ?" If you want to stretch yourself, memorize one. Stretch your brain and your ability to see by "working in" these holy descriptions of God.

The Gospels—Matthew, Mark, Luke, or John

When we want to know what God is like, we look at Jesus. When people are frustrated or distracted by so much debate over theology and doctrine (huddling in our camps) or disgruntled by Christians and the state of the Church in general, I often say, "Stop. Just stop. Stop thinking. Stop working so hard and look at Jesus. Go back to the Gospels and look at Him again." Why? Because each Gospel holds the accounts and words of Jesus, and *"Jesus is the image of the invisible God"* (Colossians 1:15).

In the Gospels we see a plethora of accounts that reveal God's attributes: servant, provider, healer, friend, peace, truth, light, shepherd, gate, etc. Take *one* aspect that you see in a passage and hone in on it for a while. A few minutes, a day, a week, a year, whatever.

Let's take an example from the Gospel of Mark: *"As Jesus walked beside the sea of Galilee, he saw Simon and his brother Andrew casting a net into the lake, for they were fishermen. 'Come follow me,' Jesus said, 'and I will send you out to fish for people'"* (Mark 1:16, 17).

Can you picture Him in the scene? What do you see?

In these two verses, I see Jesus as initiator. God calls out to humanity, in the body of Jesus, echoing Genesis 3. So as you move through the course of your day—running kids to soccer practice, in the mammogram waiting room, sipping a latte as you wait for a friend—pay attention as He initiates with you. If you think of Him, that's God initiating something with you.

Is it a discussion around something your mother-in-law ticked you off about? Curiosity about why that friend never calls? Why you're the one that always has to do the reaching out? Trust that God is initiating and calling you to see Him in that place. Over time you'll more quickly see God as Initiator.

2.   Music

Music opens our spiritual eyes like little else. Read out loud the opening verse to "Survival Plan" by Wallace and Rachel Faagutu.

"Survival Plan"

His eyes are like blazing fire

His feet are like burnished bronze

His voice is the sound of many water falls

Jesus the Lamb of God (The precious Lamb of God)[47]

Again, it's so visual! You're able to picture Him. Listen to this and other songs however you'd like, but get the lyrics out. Sing them or just read the lyrics to help with spiritual eyesight.

The Hymns

I love the iconic hymns. Think about how the Church has been inspired to see and worship God over the years with hymns like "Crown him with many crowns, the Lamb upon his throne!" Who cares what style of music is used. We all have our preferences here. If you lived in, say Iran, and found only a handful of Christians clinging to each other in the underground church, you wouldn't care one iota about the style of music. You'd just be glad you found others who love and want to worship God. Don't get caught in the trap of demanding your preferences. Most everything can lead you to see Jesus, the Glorious One!

Here's one final song.

Lover

Deepening the experience of seeing God, I find it helpful to visualize Him sitting across from me where we meet each morning.

One morning I sat in my red chair, and He in the red, velvet couch across from me. I pulled out my songbook and began to sing to Him:

Fairest Lord Jesus,

Lord of all nature,

O thou of God and man the Son;

Thee will I cherish,

Thee will I honor,

Thou my soul's glory, joy and crown.

Beautiful Saviour,

Lord of the nations,

Son of God and Son of man,

Glory and honor,

Praise adoration,

Now and forevermore be Thine. (Anon.)

I was singing right to Him. As though looking right at Him. I leaned forward, telling Him something so important I needed to get out of me. "Glory and honor" came 'round and I threw my hands in the air. Could I actually see Him? No. But I sensed His smile. His delight. My response? Tears and deep, deep joy.

I got up from my seat and moved to the small couch across from me. I curled up in it, seeing Him there with arms ready to hold me. My heart saw Him. When it did, adoration was inevitable. Beautiful Savior. Seeing Him is an experience. It's intimate and evokes feelings.

3. Feelings

Feelings got a bad rap for a long time in the Church. They were the last things to consider. I get why that was the case. It's easy to justify lots of things based on your feelings. "I've never felt so alive and in love" can be justification for walking away from your kids and husband because of an affair. Sure it feels good. There are all kinds of reasons why that's the case.

In an effort to avoid these erratic feelings with potential for unscrupulous results, we began to count them unreliable. Today, while we know that feelings aren't enough of a barometer, we know that they do in fact matter. (Those of us who lead with their heart could've told you that!) Emotional Intelligence is thought of much more highly today. Once upon a time, it was all about IQ. Now EQ (Emotional Quotient, which is your ability to perceive and apply emotional engagement) weighs in big time.

Heart Burn

This passage from Luke illustrates it well: *"When he was at the table with them, he took bread, gave thanks, broke it and began to give it to them. Then their eyes were opened and they recognized him, and he disappeared from their sight. They asked each other, 'Were not our hearts burning within us while he talked with us on the road and opened the Scriptures to us?'"* (Luke 24:30-32).

Oftentimes our bodies respond before our mind hopefully kicks into gear. Of course, for some the opposite is true. It starts in their head—rational and cognitive—before it, hopefully, drops down to the heart.

Do you always feel something? No. We can't depend on feelings *only*, but we certainly don't want to ignore when we're emotionally awakened. Emotions always inform us of something. They're powerful and can lead to understanding or *seeing*.

What Was That?

You know the feeling of something tingling down your back or hairs raised on your arms? You think, "Whoa, what was that? What's going on here?" These physical responses to our emotions—gasping at the sky's hues, heart racing over a beyond-belief performance of a gifted musician—can lead to spiritually "seeing" God's outrageous beauty.

Remember that fabulous scene in the Jim Carey version of *How the Grinch Stole Christmas*, when the Grinch realizes that Christmas must be about more than lights, stockings, and Who Pudding? He has a reaction: his arms flail about. He awkwardly trips over his own feet, holding his throbbing heart he then blurts out to his dog, "Max, help me. I'm *feeling!*" Then he sobs and sobs. Maybe the extent of your emotional expression hasn't been so dramatic. But when you have any level of heart awakening, let it draw you to God.

Scripture, music, and feelings are just three ways we can experience The Glorious One. Other ways are embedded within: Nature, people, art, science, the sky's the limit! Just stay open and pay attention. He always shows up.

CHAPTER 21

I See!

"I have seen this love. Indeed, every day I feel myself more occupied with him."
—*Catherine of Genoa*[48]

The more we practice awareness of God and His glory, the more we see God revealing Himself. This inspires belief. For many across the globe today, and during the early years of Christianity, seeing miracles, signs, and wonders inspired belief. I never want to discount people actually seeing Him with their eyes, as I believe I did as a little girl. Some of my Middle Eastern friends' powerful testimonies of coming to follow Jesus were when they actually saw Him. Like *saw* saw. But believing also stimulates seeing. It works both ways.

Seeing is Believing. Believing is Seeing

The more you look for Him, the more you'll find Him in the most unexpected places. You may be thinking, *I can believe all sorts of things that aren't really happening or imagine things that really aren't there.* But here's how I see it: I'd rather be a fool and believe that God is revealing Himself—and maybe overshoot at times—than play it cool and savvy and miss Him. Put yourself in the humble, childlike position of being on the lookout for Him. The more you look, the more you'll see. The more you see, the *more* you'll see!

But seeing God is not the end goal. We have to respond.

"I Don't Have to Do Anything With Jesus"

After speaking in Albania a couple of years ago, I flew home through Istanbul. I sat beside a woman who got chatting with me. Truth be told, I didn't want to chat. I was exhausted. As it turns out she was a Muslim who, after discovering what I do for work, said something unexpected

"I had a vision of Jesus."

"You did?" I believed her. "Tell me about it."

She went on to describe his dark hair and wheat-colored linen sash that draped across his shoulder.

I asked her, "What did you do with what you saw?"

"Nothing." She told me. I don't have to do anything with Jesus."

I was dumbfounded. And envious actually. How I'd *love* to have Him show up in a vision today. Wouldn't you?

I simply said to her, "Wow. I can tell you that if God visits you like that, He's calling you to Himself. That's an incredible gift that not everyone gets."

See, you can see and not "see." Many have.

But not you.

Respond

We take in His appearances, and the reality of His fingerprints all over the universe, and they cause our minds to swivel and swirl. They mess with us. It happens in a split second or over time, but one thing's for sure: encounters with God require a response.

We were created to respond favorably to God's glory. And when we do, here's what happens: there's a release of increase glory over and through our lives. Awakened glory must flow out!

Look at the responses to God's glory found among biblical figures:

Simeon: *"Simeon took him* (the long awaited infant Messiah) *in his arms and praised God, saying: 'Sovereign Lord, as you have promised, you may now dismiss your servant in peace. For my eyes have seen your salvation, which you have prepared in the sight of all nations: a light for revelation to the Gentiles, and the glory of your people Israel"'* (Luke 2:28-32.)

Anna: *"Coming up to them* (Mary, Joseph and the infant Messiah) *at that very moment, she gave thanks to God and spoke about the child to all who were looking forward to the redemption of Jerusalem"* (Luke 2:38).

Like Simeon, the eighty-four-year-old prophet had faithfully watched and waited for just this moment. She gasped and gazed when she saw Jesus.

A Blind Man: *"Jesus said, 'You have now seen him; in fact, he is the one speaking with you.' Then the man said, 'Lord, I believe,' and he worshiped him"* (John 9:37-38).

Mary Magdalene: *"At this, she turned around and saw Jesus standing there, but she did not realize that it was Jesus. He asked her, 'Woman, why are you crying? Who is it you are looking for?' Jesus said to her, 'Mary.' She turned toward him and cried out in Aramaic, 'Rabboni'!"* (John 20: 14).

Mary evidently then threw her arms around Jesus and intensely held on to him.

Ezekiel: *". . . the heavens were opened and I saw visions of God . . . So I got up and went out to the plain. And the glory of the LORD was standing there, like the glory I had seen by the Kebar River, and I fell facedown"* (Ezekiel 1:1, 3:23).

Job: *"My ears had heard of you but now my eyes have seen you. Therefore I despise myself and repent in dust and ashes"* (Job 42:5, 6).

Isaiah: *". . . I saw the LORD , high and exalted, seated on a throne; and the train of his robe filled the temple. . . . the doorposts and thresholds shook and the temple was filled with smoke. 'Woe to me!' I cried. 'I am ruined! For I am a man of unclean lips!'"* (Isaiah 6:1-5).

Restoration

Notice when people responded to seeing His glory with repentance, He never left them where they were. He brought them to restoration then took them to a whole new level of life. Job was transformed then blessed with a double portion, and Isaiah rose up, was commissioned by God, and sent out in power!

Scripture also gives many accounts of people walking away and doing nothing with what they saw, like the woman I met on the plane from Istanbul. There was no level of spiritual vision, resulting in little to no glory realized.

Here's additional excitement: In each of these examples, (among a whole host of others) a direct result of seeing God was worship, then stepping into the reality of who they were.

- Mary loved passionately.
- Ezekiel stood up and spoke boldly.
- Simeon finally saw what he spent his life waiting for and was ready to move on.
- Anna preached and proclaimed.
- Isaiah and Job saw their inadequacy then God raised them to whole new levels of calling equipped with a sense of awe.

Agree With God

Worship, then becoming who we were created to be, are high impact responses to seeing God. The more you really see God, the more you'll see yourself, your *true* self. The more you see your true self, the more you'll see and know God.

In the response is an agreement with God about what's been seen. It's truth about who God is. You don't *really see* God and not respond in a way that fulfills truth. Here's why: God is Truth and Light. Try regularly opening yourself up to those two basics of who God is and not see.

We can tell when a white woman's been in the sun. She's sun-kissed. We can tell when someone's had her sights on God. She exudes—whether quietly and simply, demonstratively and colorfully, or somewhere in between—a glory. It's inevitable.

It flows from seeing and responding to, God.

Cycle of Glory

If you're a mom, think about the moments you've looked into your little one's eyes and whispered, "I can't believe you're mine." You're overwhelmed with beauty. And gratitude.

That's a "seeing" moment that naturally leads to worship of God. That child? A gift that started with God. Praise and gratitude must return to God. A "you are absolutely breathtaking, Lord," or "you never, *never* cease to amaze me" response. It's not contrived. It's authentic, honest-to-goodness worship.

Glory has come full circle.

CHAPTER 22

Arise, Shine!

"Arise, shine, for your light has come, and the glory of the LORD rises upon you." —Isaiah 60:1

Approximately seven hundred years before Jesus arrived on planet earth in the flesh, the people of Israel were walking in darkness. These were God's people. The circumstances were ripe for cynicism and desperation.

They were divided: Two of the twelve tribes made up the Southern Kingdom of Judah. Ten tribes made up the Northern Kingdom of Israel. Israel had been oppressed by the surrounding powers of the Assyrians. During that time they'd fallen into idolatry, teased and tempted by political power.

At first the prophet cried out to God's people: "Look at your sin. Confess. Turn." But by chapter sixty, the tone changed.

Arise

At that point, Isaiah lifted them up with the promise of future glory: *"Arise, shine, for your light has come, and the glory of the LORD rises upon you"* (Isaiah 60:1).

By the very breath of God, Isaiah spoke of the light of the world penetrating the planet. Light bursting into darkness! He spoke of Jesus—the supreme Glorious One!

Now fast-forward seven hundred years to when Jesus informed His disciples, *"You are the light of the world"* (Matthew 5:14).

Re-Present

Pastor Bill Johnson of Bethel Church in California touches on a critical link between the two passages. According to Bill Johnson, we need to notice that Jesus didn't say, "You're *like* the light." He said, "You *are* the light."[49]

He also didn't say, "Arise, reflect." He said, "Arise, shine."

He's right. Christians often use the word *reflection* with one dictionary definition in mind: "a throwing back of light from a surface."[50] We strive to give a strong *impression* of Jesus. We try to *resemble* Him.

But these texts say that we shine. We are shining, dazzling reproductions. Why?

Because Christ is actually in us.

Take that in. In all that you are, and all that you do, you are *re*-presenting Christ.

And what's the result? What happens when you confidently and boldly carry this light, this glory? *"Nations will come to your light ... "* (Isaiah 60:3).

All Nations

North America is full of the nations. They've come to the land, but will they come to our light? Will we offer them the genuine Good News or an American version of it?

Is the Church ready to be a glorious light that draws them, not just to our land, but to the Lord?

Not if we stay huddled in our camps. Not while we slop around in the bad news.

As the people of God, if we divide and devour because of our differences, how on earth will we ever be able to love a world of people so varied and in desperate need?

The Call

God's light and life go out to all creation. It's a constant, perpetual call that originates in that Genesis 3 scene.

Knowing God—relating to and experiencing Him—is life! By enjoying His company and seeking His face, we become very much alive in Him. Then we carry His presence. The more we know God and carry His divine glory, the more we cannot help but make Him known. It's inevitable.

We reveal God to that crazy cousin. We reveal Him to our belligerent colleague. And the more we make Him known, the more alive we become.

When was the last time you watched the light go on for someone who didn't know Christ? They got it! And you were part of it. It's a high! And that is life.

Picture the Church alive:

- Truth Protectors joyfully and lovingly upholding Truth.
- The Untapped, (now Tapped) bringing a humility and welcome that's palpable.
- The Keepin' It Reals driving us back to authenticity and grace.
- Our #Blessed abuzz with a glorious hope and faith few can rival.

As we respond to God's call to life, we will be radiant. And He will be irresistible.

Thy Kingdom Come

What's the bottom line of all this talk of glory and life?

To quote Handel's *Messiah*: "The kingdom of this world is become the kingdom of our Lord and of His Christ!" ("The Hallelujah Chorus").[51]

This is the final stage in the Gospel. It's the restoration of God's original vision. Of God's kingdom. His call to all creation, "You were meant to live," will be fully realized once more!

But, dear Christian, don't hold your breath and wait until that day. Don't hunker down until this time is passed. Move out in Life!

Wherever you place your glory-drenched self, you carry and establish the kingdom of God.

Imagine, wherever there's been curse, we bring blessing.

Where there's death, we breathe life.

Imagine moving toward difficult situations in love carrying kingdom presence, power, and authority.

We call out the kingdom in a child: "Arise, shine!"

We pray it forth in our teens and Millennials: "Arise, shine!"

Thy kingdom come here, and here, and here! Until . . .

"The kingdom of this world is become the kingdom of our Lord and of His Christ."

(All rise.)

Hallelujah!

CHAPTER 23

A Glory Story

"But because of his great love for us, God, who is rich in mercy, made us alive with Christ ..." —Ephesians 2:4

Whehen our younger son, Aaron, turned sixteen, to celebrate we took him with a few friends to see his all-time favorite band.

All Things Switchfoot

Aaron loved Switchfoot and all things Switchfoot. All through his preteen and teen years, Aaron breathed the fabulous music of this band that had mentored him. Drum sets, keyboards, microphones, recording equipment, and guitar-lined walls made up our basement. And much of what Switchfoot wrote, Aaron learned, memorized, and performed.

On concert night, as we piled into the van to head into Philadelphia, one of Aaron's friends delayed in the driveway, on his knees and hunched over poster board.

"Rob, what're you doing?" we yelled. "Get in the van!"

Jumping in, he showed us the big, bold message written in chubby markers:

IT'S MY BIRTHDAY. CAN I PLAY "STARS" WITH YOU?

I remember thinking, *Who asks to perform with the band? That's pretty bold. It'd be nice, but what're the chances?*

We arrived at the Electric Factory in downtown Philly. As much as I'd have loved standing on the main floor with the kids for about four hours, Cam and I sat up in the balcony. Perfect view *and* comfortable seats. After two warm-up bands, the lights went out, and the crowd roared when Switchfoot finally took the stage.

But before we go any further, this needs one more piece of background.

Release Him, God

From the time Aaron was little, he struggled with sharing what was going on inside him. If he was hurt, afraid, angry, whatever, the tears would flow, but he could not seem to form words to share what was going on. One year, I sat with him daily after school for extended periods of time.

"If you want to talk, Aaron, I'm right here," I'd say. "I'm listening, honey. I really care about what's going on in you. I'm so sorry you're hurting."

When he was in elementary school, Aaron would sometimes walk like a little toy soldier, knees barely bending, arms stiff as though marching. He wasn't always this uptight, and it was something Cam and I prayed about quite a bit. "Release him, God. Set Aaron free to be the kid, the young man you've called him to be."

But when Aaron was alone or playing his music, he relaxed. He cut loose and we got to see who he really was. He was inspiring.

So, somewhere deep inside we held out hope that the band would see the sign and invite him up.

A Different Song

The second song Switchfoot played that night was "Stars." *Well, that's that,* I thought. *Poor Aaron, but it's still an amazing night.* From where we were perched in the balcony, we could see our group of guys mixed in with the rest of the fanatics on the floor.

Then it happened. Several songs in, inching toward the end of the concert, Jon Foreman stopped playing and hauled out of the crowd and up, onto the stage a wavy-haired kid. Throughout the concert Aaron had continued to periodically hold up his sign: **IT'S MY BIRTHDAY. CAN I PLAY 'STARS' WITH YOU?** He'd finally caught Jon Foreman's eye.

Jon lifted his own guitar strap from around his neck and placed the guitar in Aaron's hands.

"It's not 'Stars,' but it's still your birthday, right? What's your name?"

"Aaron."

"Ladies and gentleman, this is Aaron."

We all hooted and hollered like mad!

Aaron began to play one of their signature songs "Awakening."[52]

He rocked it out with the band! He came alive like the Aaron we knew was in that sixteen-year-old frame. Jumping in the air, landing on the downbeat, taking command of the stage, hair flying! We all freaked out, hooting and hollering and cheering him on! There he was up with his hero, his mentor from afar. Today, Aaron still holds that this was one of the most pivotal moments of his life.

But Up In The Balcony

That's what was happening in front of the crowd at the Electric Factory that night. Here's what was simultaneously going on in the balcony:

As soon as we realized what was happening, Cam, my analytical, businessman husband stood up, lunged forward leaning way over the railing and yelled—I mean *yelled*—over and over: "AA-RON! AA-RON! Go AARON, GO! Go AARON, GO!" Red faced, tears pouring, his dad didn't give a rip about anyone. His eye was on his kid who was alive and doing his thing!

"Go Aaron, go!"

I was catapulted into a conundrum: thrilled for Aaron but stunned by Cam. My perfectly poised husband was wrecked at the sight of the freedom and vigor of his son. Cam cheered that kid on like I've never seen him cheer in twenty-nine years of marriage. Never. All dignity—gone. It was mesmerizing.

After I quickly got over my ridiculous instinct to quiet him down (I was embarrassed. Can you imagine?), I had a holy moment in the Electric Factory.

It's You

All I could think for a few swirling moments with tears streaming down my face was, *God? Daddy? Is that what you're like with us? It is, isn't it? "Go baby, go! Go, baby. GO!"* What a sight! What a revelation of God cheering on his kids as we come alive.

I still tear up to this day when I think about the song God chose for Aaron that night. Not "Stars," as we'd hoped. "Awakening."

For Aaron, for you, me, God's glorious Church, and all people everywhere. Awakening. Because, as St. Ignatius perfectly put it, "The glory of God is man and woman fully alive."

"For from Him and through Him and to Him are all things. To Him be the glory forever! Amen" (Romans 11:36).

Final Note

I've spoken and taught on the calling of God for years. I've found that many of us struggle to take it in. That God—creator and sustainer of all—consistently and relentlessly calls us to life. To Himself. He comes looking for us, moment by moment, and habitually calls out: "Glorious one, you were meant to live."

But the struggle to see ourselves as glorious can be, well, frankly, too good to be true. But it is true.

It's true.

I pray you take this in: You, dear woman—whoever you are, wherever you are in your faith journey in seeing and following God—carry the presence, power, authority, and glory of the supreme Glorious One.

Carry it well.

Acknowledgments

First things first: Thank you, God—my Everything—for calling me to Life. I love and live for You.

Then to the fantastic people around me, who helped make this message a written reality:

Thanks to my three phenomenal men: Cam, David, and Aaron. Where would I be without you in my life? I love you men for keeping me honest and relentlessly charging me with strength and confidence.

Thanks to the Morgan James Publishing team who guided me step by step by step. I appreciate your commitment to excellence.

Thank you, Ami McConnell. I needed an editor who knew her way around the publishing block! Thanks for challenging me, cheering me on, demanding more, and becoming a friend. Thank you, Karli Jackson for your expertise in polishing it off to make the message as clear as possible.

A huge thank-you to the men and women who give of their time, gifts, and passion for Christ and His kingdom through this ministry:

- Leadership Team: Megan Boselli, Leslie Eichhorn, and Jessica Morra. I couldn't have done it without you. I love you, dear women.
- Prayer team: Byron Hawthorn, Heather Ballantine, Rebecca Emory, Craig Greenwood, Bethanne Moles, and Deneen McDonald. Affectionately known as the "Boiler Room." Thank you for

keeping prayer a core value of this ministry.

- The Board: Susan Sharp, Kathy Gendel, Cam Hicks, Alice Anderson, Dawn Griffin, and Cheryl Sparks. My guiding coalition.

Thank you to my readers: To you who bounced off ideas and unearthed God's message in me. Who read, re-read, critiqued, and challenged me. Special thanks to my lovely daughter-in-law, Rachel (bet you never thought reading my work would be part of the daughter-in-law job description!). Leslie, for applying your keen mind and big heart for Jesus, day in and day out. And Cheryl, my friend, your influence on my life is all over this book. When your time was at a premium, somehow you found enough to carry me across the finish line.

Big thank you to Danielle Strickland who wrote the foreword for this book. You lovingly and generously contributed your passion and understanding of the need for fire!

Thank you, Stacey Wei for lending your artistic expertise in your photography and the adaptation of the cross chart. Your creativity is rare.

Thank you to my friends and family who boldly confirmed God's calling on my life, which led to writing. Thank you for listening to me muse, rant, cry, and be silly. You cheered me on in it all. Hugs and high fives all 'round.

Thanks to you, dear one, for taking the time to read this, my first book. I love you and am humbled by your interest.

And finally, to Gloria, my beloved mom: I know you know.

About the Author

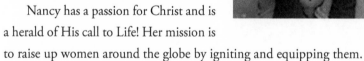

N ancy Hicks has been in communication all her life. As
an on-air spokesperson for
QVC, she inspired millions of viewers
to embrace beauty and life. After earning
her Master in Theology, she launched her
speaking ministry, NancyHicksLive.

Nancy has a passion for Christ and is
a herald of His call to Life! Her mission is
to raise up women around the globe by igniting and equipping them.

She regularly engages across the media spectrum. You can find her
speaking at conferences, on college campuses, at retreats, or via radio, televi-
sion, and social media. This is her first book.

She and Cam have been married since 1990 and have two flown-the-
coop sons, David and Aaron, and one darling daughter-in-law, Rachel.

For more information, find Nancy at nancyhickslive.com, Facebook,
and Instagram.

Endnotes

1   Os Guinness, address broadcast at Gordon College Chapel Service.

2   Glorious. (2018). Merriam-Webster. https://www.merriam-webster.com.

3   St. Augustine of Hippo, The Catechism of the Catholic Church, (354-430 AD).

4   Isaac Watts, "Alas! and Did My Saviour Bleed" (1707).

5   John Newton, "Amazing Grace" (1779).

6   Philip Yancey, What's So Amazing About Grace? (Grand Rapids: Zondervan; Visual Edition, 2003) page 12.

7   David Kinnaman, "3 Reasons Why Women Are Leaving Church," Barna Group, https://www.preachitteachit.org/articles/detail/3-reasons-why-women-are-leaving-church/.

8   Diane Paddison, "Working Women Are Leaving the Church. Here's How to Bring Them Back," Institute for Faith, Work and Economics, March 21, 2017, https://tifwe.org/working-women-are-leaving-the-church-heres-how-to-bring-them-back/.

9   Rosa Parks, Quiet Strength (Grand Rapids: Zondervan, 1994) page 22.

10 C.S. Lewis, Reflections of the Psalms (New York: Harvest/Harcourt Brace Jovanovich, 1958) page 7.

11 Dietrich Bonhoeffer, The Cost of Discipleship (New York: Macmillan Publishing Co. Inc., 1979) page 47.

12   David Brooks, The Road to Character (New York: Random House, 2015) page 54.

13   Ibid.

14   Miho Kahn, Clean Sheets, http://www.mihocleansheets.org/.

15   C. S. Lewis, Mere Christianity (Glasgow: William Collins Sons & Co. Ltd.) page 83.

16   John Piper with Desiring God Ministries. YouTube video entitled, "Prosperity Gospel"

17   Bruce Wilkinson, The Prayer of Jabez (Oregon: Multnomah Publishers Inc. 2000).

18   Nichole Nordeman , "You Make Me Want To Live" (Sony/ATV Music Publishing LLC, Capitol Christian Music Group).

19   Oswald Chambers, My Utmost for His Highest (Ohio: Barbour Publishing Inc. 1963) August 15.

20   "U.S. adults who say they regularly attend religious services continues to decline." Pew Research Center, August 1, 2018. http://www.pewforum.org/2018/08/01/why-americans-go-to-religious-services/.

21   David Kinnaman, "The State of the Church 2016." The Barna Group, 2016. https://www.barna.com/research/state-church-2016.

22   Compiled by Eric Reed. "Six Reasons Young People Leave the Church." Christianity Today, 2012. https://www.christianitytoday.com/pastors/2012/winter/youngleavechurch.html.

23   George Barna, Pennsylvania Pastor's Conference, Pennsylvania Pastor's Network, Lancaster Bible College, PA, 2016.

24   So Will I, Hillsong Joel Houston / Benjamin Hastings / Michael Fatkin.

25   Dr. David Bradstreet and Steve Rabey, Star Struck: Seeing the Creator in the Wonders of Our Cosmos (Grand Rapids: Zondervan, 2016) page 59.

26   "The Power of the Cross" by the Gettys.

27   Jack Miller, Sonship, "The Cross Chart." Used with permission by New Growth Press.

28   Soren Kierkegaard, The Prayers of Kierkergaard (Chicago: University of Chicago Press, 1956) page 21.

29   Roberta Bondi, To Love As God Loves (Minneapolis: Augsburg Fortress Publishing, 1959) page 51.

30   Randy Alcorn, Truth: A Bigger View of God's Word (Eugene: Harvest House Publishers, 2017) page 6.

31   Ella Taylor, "In 'Force Majeure,' Society Crumbles Under An Avalanche." NPR. October 24, 2014, https://www.npr.org/2014/10/24/358050035/in-force-majeure-society-crumbles-under-an-avalanche.

32   The Hebrew Greek Key Word Study Bible (AMG Publishers, 2009) page 2207.

33   Dharius Daniels. YouTube: It's A Heart Attack https://www.youtube.com/watch?v=QxufkD_ZFJg.

34   Dan Merchant. Lord, Save Us From Your Followers. Documentary. Directed by Dan Merchant. Virgil Films & Entertainment, Thunderstruck Films. 2008.

35   Excellence. (2018). Merriam-Webster. https://www.merriam-webster.com.

36   Isaac Watts, "When I Survey the Wondrous Cross" found in The Song Book of The Salvation Army (Verona, NJ: The Salvation Army National Headquarters, 1987) hymn 135, page 38.

37   Amy Carmichael, in Elisabeth Elliot's, A Chance to Die: The Life and Legacy of Amy Carmichael (Grand Rapids: Revell, 1987) page 246.

38   Richard Rohr, Falling Upward, (San Francisco, CA: Jossey-Bass, 2011) page xvii.

39   Tim Kizziar in Francis Chan, Crazy Love: Overwhelmed by a Relentless God (Colorado Springs: David C. Cook, 2013) page 93.

40   John Piper. "The Echo and Insufficiency of Hell, Part 1." Sermon Series: Behold the Kindness and Severity of God. June 14, 1992.

41   John Eldredge, Waking the Dead: The Glory of a Heart Fully Alive (Nashville: Nelson Audio 2003).

42 Regina Spektor, "Tornadoland" Sire Records, 2016.

43 Oswald Chambers, My Utmost for His Highest, (Ohio: Barbour Publishing Inc. 1963) July 7.

44 Richard Foster at Renovare's, "Making Ordinary Saints" conference held at Good Samaritan Church in Paoli, PA, September 23, 2016.

45 Beth Moore, Jesus, the One and Only (Nashville, TN: LifeWay Press, 2000) page 237.

46 Dr. Larry Crabb, interviewed in a radio broadcast.

47 Wallace and Rachel Faagutu. Survival Plan (feat. Samson). Nutu, 2009. (Used by permission.)

48 Catherine of Genoa, Devotional Classics by Richard Foster and James Bryan Smith (New York: HarperSanFriancisco, 1989) page 213.

49 Bill Johnson, Address at a Global Awakening Conference in Pennsylvania, 2016.

50 Reflection. (2018). Merriam-Webster. https://www.merriam-webster.com.

51 George Frideric Handel. Messiah from "The Hallelujah Chorus" (1741).

52 YouTube: Aaron Hicks plays "Awakening" with Switchfoot https://www.youtube.com/watch?v=jBSxpdTNvYE.

CPSIA information can be obtained
at www.ICGtesting.com
Printed in the USA
BVHW071413240319
543526BV00001B/1/P